Here is a desperately needed book for the
With the gospel under siege on every side, e
of these chapters must be heeded by all, as th
terms what is the heart of the one true, sav

Why We're Protestant deals not with peripheral issues, but with what is absolutely essential and non-negotiable to the Christian faith. You cannot be wrong here and be right with God. I urge you to devour and digest this book.

Steven J. Lawson
President, One Passion Ministries, Dallas, Texas
Teaching Fellow, Ligonier Ministries, Sanford, Florida
Professor, The Master's Seminary, Sun Valley, California

Nate's *Why We're Protestant* wonderfully demonstrates what every Christian needs at the forefront of their mind: you must be pro-Christ, pro-evangelism, pro-exposition, pro-Bible and more! My only 'protest' is that the book is too short! If you are imperatively driven, 'pick up and read.' If indicatives suit you, 'I read it with great joy.'

Mike Abendroth
Pastor of Bethlehem Bible Church
Host of No Compromise Radio

The battle for the hearts of the deceived isn't over. I'm in it every time I preach, protecting my own flock from those who would twist the Word of God. Nate's book is a helpful field guide, taking the reader through basic history and essential truths. His clear and concise points remind the mature and educate the learning of God's triumphant grace, and may also rescue some lost souls from the devil's snares!

Gabriel Hughes
Associate Pastor of First Baptist Church Lindale, Texas
Creator and Voice of *When We Understand The Text*

The Five Solas of the Reformation are the central pillars of the message and mission of the evangelical church, and therefore are always worthy of the attention and meditation of faithful followers of Jesus Christ. How much more appropriate to do so as we celebrate the 500th anniversary of the Reformation. And how much more necessary to do so at a time when we so desperately need that same Spirit of the Reformation to blow through our churches once again. May this introduction to those foundational tenets of evangelical religion be used of God to do just that.

Mike Riccardi
Pastor at Grace Community Church, Sun Valley, California
Assistant Professor of Theology, The Master's Seminary
Author of *Sanctification: The Christian's Pursuit of God-Given Holiness*

Some have jubilantly proclaimed that 'Luther's protest is over!' Is it over? Should it be over? In this excellent and immensely readable work, Pastor Nate Pickowicz shows the absolute necessity for the Protestant Reformation. The work that was begun 500 years ago by the Reformers is just as needed today as then. If you want to understand the issues related to Roman Catholicism and the need to speak the truth in love to Catholics, I highly commend this book to you.

Justin Peters
Evangelist, Apologist, and Author, Justin Peters Ministries

Five hundred years after the Reformation many Protestants have either forgotten or dismissed the doctrines that delivered the Reformers out of spiritual deception and religious bondage. Nate Pickowicz has done a masterful job in revisiting the importance of the Reformation and why Protestants need to keep contending for the Fives Solas that distinguish Roman Catholicism from Biblical Christianity. Nate's love and compassion for Catholics and his passion for the truth of the Gospel will encourage and equip you as you read *Why We're Protestant.*

Mike Gendron
Director of Proclaiming The Gospel

In our age of theological apathy and religious tolerance, we stand once again in desperate need of the burning and brilliant light of the gospel.

Nate Pickowicz does an excellent job of reminding us of the importance of the historic Reformation and pointing out our place in the long line of our gospel heritage.

Josh Buice
Pastor, Blogger at DeliveredByGrace.com,
Director of the G3 Conference

Nate Pickowicz has served the church well in calling us back to our Reformation roots. The Reformers, who married the scholar's skill with the minister's concern, would welcome the work of this bright young pastor-theologian. Pickowicz's text eloquently surveys the explosive biblical doctrines restored to glorious color, and ecclesial practice, in Europe five centuries ago. *Why We're Protestant* draws our attention once more to the Wittenberg door and reminds us that it is not a dead-end, a locked gateway, but an entrance into the world of theistic delights.

Owen Strachan
Provost and Research Professor of Theology,
Grace Bible Theological Seminary, Conway, Arkansas
Author of *Christianity and Wokeness*

Why We're Protestant is a book with several goals, all of which are combined and all of which are accomplished. This book reads like the Sports Center Highlights of the Protestant Reformation. What Pickowicz accomplishes is exceptional. Unlike many books written about the Five Solas, this one intentionally avoids Christian jargon, and would be a helpful evangelistic resource. This would be a good book to give to family members who are still in the Catholic Church. It is direct but patient, clear but kind. Most of all it is persuasive.

Jesse Johnson
Teaching Pastor, Immanuel Bible Church, Springfield, Virginia
Writer at The Cripplegate

In the ecumenical movement (including Roman Catholicism, liberal Protestantism and sectors of Eastern Orthodoxy) there is a widespread sentiment that the Reformation is over. Our age resonates less and less with theological distinctions when thinking about 'Christianity'. Pope

Francis has suggested that Christianity is like a 'polyhedron' where everything is related with everything else with no criteria. I commend Nate Pickowicz's book because it underlines the reality that the historical events of the Protestant Reformation in the sixteenth century were shaped by theological concerns that have permanent and on-going significance. Our age (and our churches) need to hear afresh why we are Protestant.

Leonardo De Chirico
Pastor of the church Breccia di Roma
Lecturer in Historical theology at Istituto di Formazione Evangelica e Documentazione (Padova, Italy) and director of the Refomanda Iniatiative

This is a refreshing and compelling presentation of the heart of Biblical Christianity: the five Solas of the Protestant Reformation. Such clear proclamation of Gospel truth is desperately needed in our age; we are led to rejoice in our great salvation, and warned of the dangers of deviating from this true path.

Bill James
Principal, London Seminary, London, UK

Nate Pickowicz

Why We're **PROTESTANT**

The Five Solas of the Reformation, and Why They Matter

CHRISTIAN
FOCUS

Copyright © Nate Pickowicz 2022

paperback ISBN 978-1-5271-0912-4
ebook ISBN 978-1-5271-0984-1

10 9 8 7 6 5 4 3 2 1

First published in 2017

This edition published in 2022
by
Christian Focus Publications, Ltd.
Geanies House, Fearn,
Ross-shire, IV20 1TW, Scotland.
www.christianfocus.com

Cover design by Rubner Durais

Printed and bound by
Bell & Bain, Glasgow

Contents

For Harvest Bible Church—

Praise God for your fellowship, love,

and hunger for the Truth

Preface to the New Edition

I minister at a small, rural church in northern New England—the hotbed of theological liberalism and post-Christian dead orthodoxy. For those seeking to find a home church, the search is often difficult and disappointing. Most New England towns have at best a church or two, but it's often a roll of the dice when you walk in the door as to what you will find. Will you find the gospel? Will there be spiritual encouragement? Will there even be Christians in attendance, or is it simply a social club?

A few years ago, in conjunction with the Protestant celebration of the 500th anniversary of the Reformation, I published a shorter version of the book you now hold in your hands. As I considered the distinguishing markers of the Christian faith, it struck me that so few Protestants I knew were confident understanding or explaining the core tenets of the Protestant faith. I wanted to offer some help. The result was *Why We're Protestant: An Introduction to the Five Solas of the Reformation.*

In the kindness of God, the book was well-received. Suddenly, I was getting emails and letters from people around the world sharing the impact the book had had on them. Some gave copies away to unsaved family and friends. Others used it as an apologetic tool. While others simply read it to help them further understand what they believe.

Since its release, however, I have felt like I wanted to say a bit more. When Christian Focus approached me with the prospect of publishing with them, I leapt at the opportunity to release a more definitive edition of *Why We're Protestant*. This new volume has not only been revised from the original, but I have added three appendices that are designed to expand on some key Protestant themes: the priesthood of all believers, the theology of the cross, and *simul justus et peccator*. It's my hope that this book will serve as a helpful introductory resource for believers everywhere to be able to give a defense of biblical Christianity and the Protestant position. May the Lord bring glory to Himself and edify His church through this work.

Nate Pickowicz
March 2022

Introduction
The Protestant Crisis

We are currently in the midst of a crisis. On the surface, it appears to be a Protestant crisis but, in truth, it's more of a *Christianity* crisis. The tenets of the Christian faith are under attack by the very same people who claim to be upholding them. Sadly, many people who regularly sit in 'Christian' churches believe they are going to heaven, but they are being taught a message that will surely not lead them there. While Jesus said, 'I am the way, the truth, and the life; no one comes to the Father, through Me' (John 14:6), scores of churchgoers are being told that eternal life is attained by other means. Therefore, this is most certainly a *gospel* crisis. And for five hundred years, it has been clear that Protestants and Catholics have two different understandings of: what is the gospel, how a person gets right with God, and how to get to heaven.

Recently, however, the Protestant Church has been drifting back toward Rome. In earlier years, the Roman Catholic Church made no bones about the division between the two groups, but since Vatican II (1962–1965), the world has believed it was seeing a 'kinder, gentler' Catholic Church. In 1994, a number of prominent Protestant and Catholic leaders signed an ecumenical document called Evangelicals and Catholics Together (ECT). While this effort was met with much resistance on both sides, it was a sign that the times were changing. Even today, many Protestants have linked arms with Roman Catholics, thus presenting to the world a unified religious front.

However, Protestantism and Roman Catholicism are two completely opposing religious systems. While they use much of the same theological language, their understanding of the person of God, the nature of sin, the work of Jesus Christ, the gospel, the doctrines of justification and sanctification, the church, the content and authority of the Scriptures, and the Christian mission is completely different. Yet there are Protestants who muddy the waters by pretending that no such distinction exists.

WHY IS THIS HAPPENING?

The problem is multi-faceted. The spirit of our present age is one of so-called 'tolerance'—a blind acceptance of all worldviews and religions (except for biblical Christianity!), regardless of the validity of their truth-claims. Liberalism is surging, and ecumenism is on the rise. Many Christians seem to believe that since both Catholics and Protestants use much of the same language ('God,' 'Jesus,' 'Church,' 'Bible,' etc.), the two groups are 'close enough' and everyone who claims the name of Christ should set aside their differences and accept one another in faith. But this attitude is both careless and intellectually dishonest.

Further compounding the problem, biblical and theological literacy is at a new low.[1] Frankly, many Protestants don't know what the Bible says, nor what they should believe. Modern-day mysticism has swept professing Christians into the belief that if something feels right, then it is. Therefore, they maintain that the rejection

---

1. Many recent studies have shown this fact to be true. One of the more helpful articles to address the phenomenon is Chris Larson, 'The State of Theology: New Findings on America's Theological Health,' http://www.ligonier.org/blog/state-theology-new-findings-americas-theological-health/ (accessed July 21, 2017).

of Roman Catholic dogma is wrong, simply because it feels like it should be wrong.

Beyond this, Protestants are growing increasingly ignorant of the gospel. Because of their lack of biblical knowledge, mixed with lowest-common-denominator credos like, 'Just love Jesus,' etc., they are largely ignorant of what it actually means to be a Christian—namely, the belief in the saving gospel of Jesus Christ laid out in the Scriptures. This sort of minimalist-Christianity is eating Protestantism like cancer. In short, Protestants don't know why they're Protestants.

Making matters worse, much of mainstream Protestantism has been held captive to sensationalism and easy-believism. The popularity of the seeker church movement has effectively created a shallow faith experience for many believers. Growing tired of being shown 'what's new,' this generation of Christians has found themselves untethered to anything resembling an historic Christianity. The veneer is starting to peel off, and Christians are looking to fall back toward a more seemingly traditional faith. Out of discontent and fatigue, many disenfranchised Protestants are wandering off the megachurch reservation, and crossing the Tiber into the arms of Mother Mary.

These, and other reasons, are why a re-examination of the core of Protestant Christianity is desperately needed.

Why the Reformation Happened

At the height of Rome's corruption, a movement took shape in the sixteenth century to reform the Church. Men like Martin Luther, Philip Melanchthon, Ulrich Zwingli, John Calvin, John Knox, William Tyndale, and others, were used by God to recapture what had been lost for a thousand years—the essentials of biblical Christianity. Like Moses, David, and Paul, these men were far from perfect: Luther was known for his ungracious attitude toward non-believers, Zwingli was enamored with nationalistic zeal (he died on the battlefield, sword-in-hand!), and Calvin has been deemed guilty-by-association in the death of Michael Servetus. But despite having feet of clay, God used these men to bring about a worldwide Reformation, and open the doors for the gospel to be spread to all corners of the earth.

What was the message of the Reformation? In essence, the main question asked and answered was: *How does a person get right with God?* This was the central issue. For Rome, sinners are saved by faithfully adhering to the dogma of the Catholic Church. But when the Reformers began to examine the Bible, they saw that salvation came by God Himself through the gospel of Jesus Christ. And while the totality of Reformation doctrine was vast (see John Calvin's *magnum opus Institutes of the Christian Religion*), the spirit of the Reformation comes to us through five credos known as, 'The Five *Solas'*—*sola Scriptura, sola gratia, sola fide, solus Christus,* and *soli Deo gloria.*

The Content and Aim of This Book

In the spring of 2017, I had the privilege of teaching through *The Five Solas* at Harvest Bible Church in Gilmanton Iron Works, New Hampshire. Very quickly, I realized that my six-week series could have easily been a sixty-week series, as the material was so dense and wondrously rich! Admittedly, my contribution will, at best, serve as a mere introduction to a broader field of Reformation theology and literature. In fact, I would encourage the reader to access the Bibliography at the end of this book to find further resources for study.

But in approaching the topic of the Protestant Reformation in this book, we will examine the question: *How does a person get right with God?* In the end, my hope for this book is that it would help re-drive the nail into Wittenberg's door. May this serve as a reminder to those who have forgotten and an apologetic to those who are unconvinced. Above all, may Jesus Christ be exalted and the Lord God be glorified!

Soli Deo Gloria!

... the righteousness of God is revealed from faith for faith:as it is written, 'The righteous shall live by faith.'
(Romans 1:17)

1.
Light After Darkness:
Origins of the Protestant Reformation

Post tenebras lux! It is a Latin phrase translated 'light after darkness,' adopted in Geneva as the motto of the Protestant Reformation. After nearly a thousand years of oppressive Church rule, aptly referred to as 'the dark ages,' the Reformation brought to light the truths of biblical Christianity, rescuing the saving gospel from obscurity. While 2017 has been recognized as the 500th anniversary of Martin Luther posting his Ninety-Five Theses in Wittenberg, it is important to note that the Reformation did not begin with Luther *per se*. There were tremors being felt all throughout Europe in the centuries before.

Early Tremors of Reformation
The Waldensians
In the latter days of the twelfth century, a man named Peter Waldo (1140–1205) launched a grassroots spiritual movement, challenging the beliefs and practices of the Roman Catholic Church. What came to be known as 'the Waldensian movement' was marked by several things; chiefly lay preaching, simple living, and a strict adherence to the Bible. Waldo himself is credited with providing the first European Bible translation into a modern language. After being excommunicated in 1184, Peter Waldo and

his disciples fled to the mountains of northern Italy where they lived out the rest of their days in hiding.

John Wycliffe

Nearly two centuries later, a seminary professor at Oxford named John Wycliffe (1320–1384) opposed the abuses of Roman Catholic priests. Out of love for the body of Christ, and realizing the great need for a Bible translation for regular people, Wycliffe undertook the immense task of translating the Bible from the Latin Vulgate into Middle English in 1382. However, this immediately placed a target on his back, as Rome feared their loss of authority and influence, should 'commoners' learn the Scriptures and push back against the abuses. As time went on, Wycliffe became even more convinced of the corruption of the priests, the error of Roman Catholic doctrine, and the invalidity of the papacy. He died a hated man at age sixty-four; the council of Constance posthumously declared him a heretic in 1415. Later, in 1428, Wycliffe's remains were exhumed, burned, and scattered into the River Swift in England.

John Hus

Another pre-Reformation leader was a Bohemian scholar named John Hus. Heavily influenced by the writings of Wycliffe, Hus carried on his message, declaring that the teachings of the Roman Catholic Church were contrary to the teaching of Scripture. His popularity grew throughout all of Europe, and Rome was eager to shut him down. When asked whether he was willing to obey the commands of the Pope, Hus replied, 'Yes, so far as they agree with the doctrine of Christ, but when I see the contrary I will not obey them, even though you burn my body.'[1] In the end, he was excommunicated, tried, imprisoned, and finally burned at the stake on June 7, 1415.

---

1. S.M. Houghton, *Sketches from Church History* (Edinburgh: Banner of Truth, 1980), 69.

For years, many challenged the abuses and false doctrines of the Catholic Church, but all were silenced. However, there would be one voice that would not be silenced.

Martin Luther

Martin Luther was born in Eisleben, Germany on November 10, 1483 to Hans and Margaret Luder ('Luther' is the Latinized rendering). Although his family were peasants, his father worked very hard to provide Martin with the chance to earn a good education. Hans Luther wanted better for Martin than a life in the coal mines, so he sent him away to school to become a lawyer. He would graduate from the University of Erfurt in 1505 with Bachelor's and Master's degrees under his belt. He was ready to take the study of the law by storm, but it would be the Lord who would take Martin by storm.

On July 2, only a few months after graduation, Martin was returning home from Erfurt when he was caught in a terrible thunderstorm. Growing up with a mother who was deeply devout and superstitious, he was prone to see every event of life as having spiritual significance. For him, the thunderstorm was nothing less than God's unleashing of judgment on his soul. Suddenly, a bolt of lightning pierced the clouds and knocked him to the ground. In sheer terror, Martin cried out to the patron saint of miners, 'Help me, Saint Anne, and I will become a monk!' This would prove to be one of many turning points in the life of Martin Luther. His biographer, noting the providential irony of the event, writes:

> The man who thus called upon a saint was later to repudiate the cult of the saints. He who avowed to become a monk was later to renounce monasticism. A loyal son of the Catholic Church, was later to shatter the structure of medieval Catholicism. A devout servant of the Pope, he was later to identify the Popes with Antichrist.[2]

---

2. Roland H. Bainton, *Here I Stand: A Life of Martin Luther* (Peabody: Hendrickson, 1950), 1.

Two weeks later, Martin announced that he was giving up his doctoral studies in law, and making good on his promise to become a monk. His father was furious. As Luther records, 'When I became a monk, my father almost went out of his mind. He was all upset and refused to give me his permission.'[3] Martin would go anyway.

The Terror of God

Of the seven monasteries in Erfurt, Luther chose one of the more strict—the Augustinian order. He had hoped that his devotion to monastic life would ensure a life of peace, as he was constantly fearful of God's judgment. And, certainly, God couldn't be displeased with a monk! Martin was determined to keep the requirements of monastic life to the letter. Recalling his days in the monastery, Luther would later write, 'If any monk ever got to heaven by monkery, then I should have made it.'[4] He was obsessive, unrelenting, and legalistic about his regimen. His slavish devotion to prayers, fasting, sleeping without blankets, punishing himself, etc., nearly cost him his life. He writes:

> I tortured myself ... and I inflicted upon myself such pain as I would never inflict again, even if I could ... if it had lasted much longer, I would have killed myself with vigils, praying, reading, and the other labors.[5]

But why such extreme behavior? Why the torturous regimen? Why the devotion to utter self-destruction? One word: sin.

Luther couldn't escape the reality of his own condition. Having previously been a law student, his mind was trained on the tiniest details of the law; and as a monk, he could not escape the exacting nature of God's holy law. And it plagued him. 'Oh, my sins! My sins! My sins!' he would cry—hysterical

---

3.   Stephen J. Nichols, *Martin Luther: A Guided Tour of His Life and Thought* (Phillipsburg: Presbyterian & Reformed, 2002), 28.

4.   ibid., 29.

5.   ibid.

over them, and laboring tireless to confess each and every one. It was not uncommon for Luther to spend several hours each day in the confessional, bearing his soul to his fellow monks. Growing ever tired of Luther's carrying on, his mentor, Johann von Staupitz, replied to him, 'Man, God is not angry with you. You are angry. Don't you know that God commands you to hope?' He continued, 'Look here, Brother Martin. If you're going to confess so much, why don't you go do something worth confessing? Kill your father or mother! Commit adultery! Quit coming here with such flummery and fake sins!'[6] But Luther couldn't rid himself of his guilt and shame over even the most minute sin.

The problem was only worsened by his first mass. For Roman Catholicism, the mass is the centerpiece of religion. In the mass, the sacraments of bread and wine become the body and blood of Jesus Christ, and are re-offered up as a sacrifice for sins. The gravity of the event cannot be overemphasized. And Luther felt the weight of it.

His father had ridden in to join his son in his first mass, along with twenty guests and a handsome gift for the monastery. The pressure on Martin couldn't have been greater. At the start of the introductory portion, he was supposed to say, 'We offer unto Thee, the living, the true, the eternal God.' However, before he could utter the words, he froze in terror. His throat closed up. His lips began to quiver. Droplets of sweat began to form on his forehead. Luther stood terrified. He later confessed:

> At these words I was utterly stupefied and terror-stricken. I thought to myself, 'With what tongue shall I address such Majesty, seeing that all men ought to tremble at the presence of even an earthly prince? Who am I, that I should lift up mine eyes or raise my hands to the divine Majesty? The angels surround him. At his nod the earth trembles. And shall I, a miserable little pigmy,

---

6. Timothy George, *Theology of the Reformers* (Nashville: B&H, 2013), 65.

say, 'I want this, I ask for that'? For I am dust and ashes and full of sin and I am speaking to the living, eternal and the true God.'[7]

He struggled to finish the mass. His father immediately fled the monastery, fuming mad with embarrassment. But that would be the least of Martin's troubles.

In an attempt to alleviate Martin from his downward spiral, his mentor Staupitz suggested to him that a trip to the Eternal City would do his soul some good. And so, in 1510, Luther made a pilgrimage to Rome. He arrived full of hope, but his hopes were dashed, as the holy city proved to be a hellish city. To his disgust and disillusionment, Luther observed the very worst from the Roman clergy. The priests were arrogant, flippant, licentious, and irreverent; many of whom were practicing the most wicked behavior fit only for pagans. Aghast, Luther wrote, 'No one can imagine the knavery, the horrible sinfulness and debauchery that are rampant in Rome.'[8] Nevertheless, he visited all the holy sites, including climbing on his knees up the stairs of Pontius Pilate, reciting the Lord's Prayer ('Our Father') on each step. The worshipers were told that if they did this, when they arrived at the top step, the soul of a loved one would be sprung from purgatory. But when Luther reached the top, he could only say, 'Who knows if this is true?'

Upon his return home, Luther was no more encouraged than before he left; in fact, he had sunk even deeper into his depression. The very things that were supposed to bring a Catholic believer hope and peace were bringing him further into the depths of despair. Frustrated, Staupitz asked Luther why he couldn't comprehend the love of God. 'Love God?' he replied, 'I can't love God, I hate him.' Unsure what else to do, Staupitz announced that Luther was being sent to the University of Wittenberg to become a teacher, which would help get his mind off his spiritual ailments. And so, in 1511,

---

7.   Bainton, *Here I Stand*, 21.

8.   Nichols, *Martin Luther*, 30.

Martin Luther traveled to Wittenberg, Germany, where he would spend the rest of his life.

The Rediscovery of the Doctrine of Justification

Upon arrival at the Augustinian monastery in Wittenberg, Luther began to work on his doctorate in theology, which he earned in 1512. Soon after being appointed to the faculty at the University, he began to teach the Bible—first the Psalms (1513–1515), then Romans (1515–1516), Galatians (1516–1517), and Hebrews (1517). These studies would constitute a paradigm shift in Luther's thinking, and through his studies, he came to the knowledge of saving faith in Jesus Christ.

While it's hard to nail down his date of conversion, we do get a glimpse of Luther's thought process, as he came to understand the gospel. Previously, Luther had only ever understood an angry, vengeful God; a terrifying image of Christ wielding a sword of divine judgment. This view of the Lord plagued him. But while teaching Psalm 22, Luther encountered another side of Christ— that of a suffering servant, abandoned by His Father, crying out, 'My God, My God, why have you forsaken Me?' This image was only intensified when Luther contemplated Christ in the Garden of Gethsemane, sweating drops of blood in anguish. And then to see the Savior, nailed to the cross, suffering the punishment of God. His understanding began to change. Luther was seeing a Christ who bore sin and judgment on Himself, dying *for him*. 'The contemplation of the cross had convinced Luther that God is neither malicious nor capricious,' writes Roland Bainton, 'But there still remains the problem of the justice of God.'[9]

When he arrived upon the text of Paul's letter to the Romans, he found himself transfixed on the phrase: 'the righteousness of God' (Rom. 1:17). In fact, Luther obsessed over it. He longed for understanding. He writes:

---

9.   Bainton, *Here I Stand*, 46.

My situation was that, although an impeccable monk, I stood before God as a sinner troubled in conscience, and I had no confidence that my merit would assuage him. Therefore I did not love a just and angry God, but rather hated and murmured against him. Yet I clung to the dear Paul and had a great yearning to know what he meant.[10]

Luther wrestled night and day, agonizing over the text, until he saw the connection between 'the righteousness of God' in Romans 1:17 and Paul's quotation of Habakkuk 2:4 just a few words later—'the just will live by faith.' The blinders started to come off. The weight was being lifted. Luther recounts:

At last, by the mercy of God, *meditating day and night*, I gave heed to the context of the words, namely, 'In it the righteousness of God is revealed, as it is written, "He who through faith is righteous shall live." There *I began to understand* [that] the righteousness of God is that by which the righteous lives by a gift of God, namely by faith. And this is the meaning: the righteousness of God is revealed by the gospel, namely, the passive righteousness with which [the] merciful God justifies us by faith, as it is written, 'He who through faith is righteous shall live.' Here I felt that I was altogether born again and had entered paradise itself through open gates. Here a totally other face of the entire Scripture showed itself to me.[11]

At one point in his life, Luther had said, 'If I could believe that God was not angry with me, I would stand on my head for joy.'[12] That day had finally come. Whereas Luther, along with the whole of Christendom, had believed that a person had to *become* righteous through sheer willpower; in truth, righteousness is *granted as a gift* by God to those who have faith in Jesus Christ.

---

10. ibid., 48.

11. John Piper, *The Legacy of Sovereign Joy: God's Triumphant Grace in the Lives of Augustine, Luther, and Calvin* (Wheaton: Crossway, 2000), 91-92.

12. ibid., 84.

At the time when Luther was exploring the riches of his new discovery—the doctrine of justification by faith—he was made aware of a great perversion of God's grace, one that needed to be opposed swiftly and vigorously: the sale of indulgences.

The Selling of Indulgences and Luther's Ninety-Five Theses

In the Middle Ages, the Roman Catholic Church developed the doctrine of purgatory—an intermediate state between heaven and hell; a place where the sinner could continue to pay for their sins and be purified by fire, in hopes of one day being sprung out and ascend to heaven. But while on earth, there were four sacraments that accomplished the forgiveness for sins and removal of guilt: *baptism*, the *Eucharist*, *penance*, and *extreme unction* (anointing the sick). The faithful observance of these was said to lessen one's time in purgatory. In Luther's day, the central practice in Catholicism was penance.

The sacrament of *penance* was an act of absolution (pardoning) of sin, and it involved three steps: contrition (sorrow over sin), confession to a priest, and satisfaction (something the sinner had to do). Once these steps were done to the priest's contentment, he would grant absolution—forgiveness of sin, release from punishment, and restoration to a good standing with God.

The basis for granting forgiveness was the belief that Christ accomplished more good works than were required by God's law. These *extra* works were then deposited into a heavenly treasury which could be dispensed to the people at the Pope's discretion. Additionally, certain noble Christian 'saints' who accomplished good works on earth would have their merits added to the treasury. There were several ways of accessing this divine treasury, including the various sacraments, as well as the viewing of religious relics on holy days. Another way was through the purchase of an indulgence.

An *indulgence* was an official document granted by the Pope that would substitute the rigorous practice of penance with a simple payment of money. In essence, sinners could now buy forgiveness. In addition to granting the penitent sinner access to the merits of the divine treasury, the sale of indulgences also provided a substantial revenue for the Roman Catholic Church. In an effort to raise money for the repair and remodeling of Saint Peter's in Rome, Pope Leo X authorized the sale of a special indulgence at the hands of a Dominican monk named John Tetzel—a high-pressure salesman, known for his unscrupulous methods of peddling his spiritual product. Tetzel boasted that his super-indulgence promised to speed up the process of penance, guaranteeing 'the complete forgiveness of all sins' for those who would make the one time purchase.

Further, the purchase of these indulgences could also be used to commute the sentence of a loved one suffering in purgatory, transferring them immediately to heaven. Tetzel even had a catchphrase: 'As soon as the coin in the coffer rings, the soul from purgatory springs.' Naturally, such a guarantee was music to the ears of the poor, guilt-ridden peasants of Germany. In fact, in some places, the demand was so high that new coins were being minted on site to be used in the coffers. Although Tetzel never came to Wittenberg, the citizens traveled to the surrounding towns to purchase indulgences. When Luther caught wind of what was taking place, he was furious. For him, Tetzel's antics were the straw that broke the camel's back. It was spiritual abuse of the worse kind, and Luther had had enough.

Springing to action, Luther penned a series of ninety-five propositions—indictments against the errors and abuses of the Catholic Church. With Romans 1:17 still fresh in his mind, Luther built his attack around the sale of indulgences, and expanded from there.

In what would come to be known as his 'Ninety-Five Theses' Luther would assert:

2. The word *repentance* cannot be understood to mean the sacrament of penance, or the act of confession and satisfaction administered by the priests.

3. Yet it does mean inward repentance only, as there is no inward repentance that does not manifest itself outwardly through various mortifications of the flesh.

6. The Pope cannot remit any guilt, except by declaring that it has been remitted by God and by assenting to God's work of remission.

21. Therefore those preachers of indulgences are in error, who say that by the Pope's indulgences a man is freed from every penalty and is saved.

28. It is certain that when the coin jingles into the money-box, greed and avarice can be increased, but the result of the intercession of the church is in the power of God alone.

36. Every truly repentant Christian has a right to full remission of penalty and guilt, even without letters of pardon.

62. The true treasure of the church is the most holy gospel of the glory and grace of God.

92. Away, then, with all those prophets who say to the people of Christ, 'Peace, peace,' and there is no peace!

94. Christians are to be exhorted to be diligent in following Christ, their Head, through penalties, death, and hell;

95. And thus be confident of entering into heaven through many tribulations, rather than through the false assurance of peace.[13]

And with that, on October 31, 1517, Martin Luther nailed his Ninety-Five Theses to the door of the castle at Wittenberg, challenging the Pope and the Roman Catholic Church to answer the charges set forth.

---

13. All excerpts quoted here are from Stephen J. Nichols, ed. *Martin Luther's Ninety-Five Theses*. Phillipsburg: Presbyterian & Reformed, 2002.

Initially, there was little response, but soon, word of Luther's bold declaration traveled throughout Germany and made its way to Rome. Stephen Nichols notes, 'At this point, and even for the next two years, Luther desired to reform the church from within, as he had no intention of breaking with it altogether. As Luther's theological understanding developed, however, he soon realized the impossibility of that approach.'[14]

The Diet of Worms

At first, the Pope dismissed Luther's writings as the musings of a drunken German. But as Luther's mass-produced writings began circulating throughout Europe, the threat became more immanent. The first debates between Luther and delegates from Rome were somewhat cordial, but the tone would soon change. Luther would debate Church leaders in Heidelberg, Augsburg, and Leipzig, before receiving a papal bull in 1520—an official document signed by the Pope declaring Luther to be an enemy of the Church. In the pronouncement, he was ordered to cease and desist from his teachings, and recant within sixty days. In response, Luther publicly burned the papal bull.

In 1521, Luther was summoned to appear in the city of Worms, to be tried for heresy. On the first day, expecting an opportunity to debate, Luther was broadsided with only two curt questions. With his writings spread out on a table in front of him, he was asked if they belonged to him. In a barely audible voice, he answered, 'The books are all mine,' but added, 'and I have written more.' All hope of launching into debate was dashed when the official posed the second question: 'Do you defend them all, or do you care to reject a part?' Unsure of how to respond, as much of what he had written was still within the bounds of Catholic orthodoxy, trembling before the court, he uttered, 'I beg you, give me time to think it over.' After a short deliberation, Luther was given one night to consider it.

---

14. Nichols, *Martin Luther*, 36.

The following day, Luther returned more composed than the previous day. As before, he was asked: 'Do you recant?' Once again, Luther attempted to discuss his views, but was swiftly shut down. The official pressed him: 'I ask you, Martin—answer candidly and without horns—do you or do you not repudiate your books and the errors which they contain?' Realizing the importance of the moment, and seeing that he would not be afforded the opportunity to explain himself, he uttered these now famous words:

> Since then your serene majesty and your lordships seek a simple answer, I will give it in this manner, not embellished: Unless I am convinced by the testimony of the Scriptures or by clear reason, for I do not trust either in the Pope or in councils alone, since it is well known that they have often erred and contradict themselves, I am bound to the Scriptures I have quoted and my conscience is captive to the Word of God. I cannot and I will not retract anything, since it is neither safe nor right to go against conscience. I cannot do otherwise, here I stand. May God help me, Amen.

And with that, Luther 'threw up his arms in the gesture of a victorious knight,'[15] and exited the hall and went into hiding. The officials then pronounced Luther a heretic and an outlaw, and placed a bounty on his head, one that would remain on him for the rest of his life.

The Birth of Protestantism

Luther's stand at the Diet of Worms was not the end, rather, merely the beginning. For the next twenty-five years, he would write, preach, pastor a church, and raise a family. But the events of 1517–1521 marked the first true break from Rome, and the Protestant Reformation was born. The Reformation would not stay only in Germany. It would soon spread to Switzerland through the work of Ulrich Zwingli, to France through John Calvin and

---

15. Bainton, *Here I Stand*, 181.

Theodore Beza, to England through William Tyndale and Thomas Cranmer, and to Scotland through John Knox.

The Five *Solas*

While the Protestant Reformation had many aspects—moral, intellectual, cultural—it was primarily a theological Reformation. Carl Trueman notes,

> [Luther's] attack on indulgences in 1517 was in large part an attack on abusive pastoral practice driven by church greed; but it was also rooted in his changing theology which saw the sale of indulgences as cheapening God's grace, trivializing sin and misleading the laity. He did not attack the practice simply because it was abusive in its practical outworkings but because it rested upon a false view of God and of humanity's status before God.[16]

At the core of the Reformation lies the central question: *How does a person get right with God?* To answer this question is to strike at the heart of the need for Christ. And in approaching this question, the Reformers would set out to rediscover and establish the bounds of essential Christianity through five declarations: *sola Scriptura* (Scripture alone), *sola gratia* (grace alone), *sola fide* (faith alone), *solus Christus* (Christ alone), and *soli Deo gloria* (the glory of God alone). With these five markers, the errors of Roman Catholicism would be refuted, and Protestantism would be established. In the coming chapters, we will explore each of the five *solas*. And, by God's grace, we will come to understand not only the Reformation, but the Christian faith itself.

---

16. Carl R. Trueman, *Reformation: Yesterday, Today and Tomorrow* (Fearn, Scotland: Christian Focus, 2000), 20.

*All Scripture is breathed out by God and profitable
for teaching, for reproof, for correction,
and for training in righteousness,
that the man of God may be complete,
equipped for every good work.
(2 Timothy 3:16-17)*

2.
Sola Scriptura
(Scripture Alone)

Within a year of posting his Ninety-Five Theses, Martin Luther was summoned to appear before Cardinal Cajetan to be examined for his accusations against the Roman Catholic Church's theology and practice. When the Cardinal pressed him on the issue of the church's authority, Luther responded, 'The truth of Scripture comes first. After that is accepted one may determine whether the words of men can be accepted as true.'[1] Now, Luther was not discrediting the words of men completely, rather, he was claiming that, far and above anything or any*one* else, Holy Scripture was first and foremost. This led to the development of *sola Scriptura*— 'Scripture alone.'

Now, before we can proceed with answering our initial question of *how a person can get right with God*, we first need to establish a foundation. It has been said that 'justification by faith alone was the *material principle* of the Reformation,' that is, it was 'at the heart of the *content* of the Reformation.' However, 'the recovery of Scripture was its *formal principle*'—in other words, *sola Scriptura* 'was at the heart of its *method*.'[2] While a right understanding of the doctrine of

---

1. Mark D. Thompson, 'Sola Scriptura,' in *Reformation Theology: A Systematic Summary*, ed. Matthew Barrett (Wheaton: Crossway, 2017), 153.

2. Michael Reeves & Tim Chester, *Why the Reformation Still Matters* (Wheaton: Crossway, 2016), 42.

justification answers the key question—*How does a person get right with God?*—as we'll see, the recovery of the doctrine of Scripture was the driving force that propelled the Reformation forward.

William Tyndale's Battle for the Bible

By the mid-1520s, the Reformation was ablaze, as the writings of Luther were finding their way into every corner of Europe. However, it was the publishing of Desiderius Erasmus' Greek New Testament in 1516 that laid the straw for the fire. For a thousand years prior to Erasmus, the church had only the Latin Vulgate for its Bible. But now, Christians were able to read the New Testament Scriptures in Greek—the original language in which they were written. This work became the basis for Luther's German Bible translation, but it would also inspire another young scholar to attempt a new translation for believers into the English language.

William Tyndale was born in a small, rural town in Gloucestershire, England, around 1494. A young man of tremendous promise, William was enrolled at Magdalen Hall, followed by Oxford and Cambridge. While in school, he displayed considerable aptitude for languages. In fact, by the end of his life, Tyndale was proficient in eight languages—Hebrew, Greek, Latin, Italian, Spanish, English, German, and French.[3] Upon graduation, William took an interest in theology, but lamented the fact that Christians were shielded from reading and understanding the Bible.

It was during his time at Oxford and Cambridge that he was drawn to the teachings of Luther and the Reformers. With the fires of Reformation raging, Tyndale became passionate about Protestantism on English soil. Since many people—laity and clergy alike—could not read or understand Latin, he realized that England could not be evangelized using the Vulgate. Therefore, he concluded, 'It was impossible to establish the lay people in any truth, except the Scripture were laid before their eyes in their

---

3. Steven Lawson, *The Daring Mission of William Tyndale* (Orlando: Reformation Trust, 2015), xx.

mother tongue.'[4] From that moment, Tyndale resolved to provide a new translation of the Bible from the original languages (Hebrew and Greek) into English—a feat never accomplished before.

At first, Tyndale proposed his new idea to the magistrates in London, but they turned him down, fearing the furtherance of Luther's controversial Reformation in England. Tyndale was shocked at the ignorance of the local priests. During a heated argument with one such priest, Tyndale exclaimed, 'I defy the Pope and all his laws!' and added, 'if God spared him life, ere many years he would cause a boy that drives the plough to know more of the Scripture than he does.'[5]

As opposition grew, Tyndale fled to Germany and Belgium, where he would undertake the work of translation. While in Germany, Tyndale likely sat under the tutelage of Martin Luther—further strengthening his resolve. In 1525, the first edition of Tyndale's English New Testament appeared. In fact, some believe that as many as three thousand copies of Tyndale's New Testament were secretly printed in the city of Worms (Luther's battleground) and then smuggled into England.[6] Seven editions of his work would be published, although only parts of the Old Testament would be finished by Tyndale himself. However, his enemies finally caught up with him. He was arrested and burned at the stake in October 1536. His last words were a plea to God, 'Oh Lord! Open the king of England's eyes!'

What was it that drove William Tyndale to risk his life to translate the Bible? Why did Martin Luther stand defiantly before the Diet of Worms and declare that his 'conscience was captive to the Word of God'?

---

4. ibid., 8.

5. *Fox's Book of Martyrs: A History of the Lives, Sufferings and Triumphant Deaths of the Early Christian and the Protestant Martyrs*, ed. William Byron Forbush (Philadelphia: John C. Winston, 1926), 178.

6. Alister McGrath, *Christianity's Dangerous Idea: The Protestant Revolution—A History from the Sixteenth Century to the Twenty-First* (New York: HarperOne, 2007), 215.

The answer: *sola Scriptura*.

But in order to examine this principle within the context of the Reformation, we first need to explore the doctrine of Scripture itself. For the rest of this chapter, we will examine four foundational claims regarding the Word of God: its *inspiration*, *inerrancy*, *authority*, and *sufficiency*.

The Issue of Inspiration

The most dynamic and explicit passage in all of Scripture about the nature of the Bible's own divine inspiration comes in 2 Timothy 3:16-17. The apostle Paul writes:

> All Scripture is breathed out by God and profitable for teaching, for reproof, for correction, and for training in righteousness, that the man of God may be complete, equipped for every good work.

In the Greek, the word *theopneustos* is used to describe how Scripture came to be; it was literally 'God-breathed.' It was as if the Lord took a deep breath in, and then exhaled Holy Scripture. Further, the means by which God brought Scripture about was through the pens of human writers—'men [who] spoke from God as they were carried along by the Holy Spirit' (2 Pet. 1:21). Both the Roman Catholic Church and the Protestant Reformers did not disagree about divine inspiration. What *was* and *is still* contested, however, is the *content* of the revelation.

Paul's use of the word 'all' in 2 Timothy 3:16 leads us to examine: *What books of the Bible are contained in the 'all' of Scripture?* This is the question of the *canon*. The word 'canon' comes from the Greek word *kanōn*, which means 'measuring rod'—which came to be used in speaking of a 'rule' or 'standard.'[7] And in the most general sense, the canon is '*the authoritative books that God gave*

---

7. F.F. Bruce, *The Canon of Scripture* (Downers Grove: InterVarsity Press, 1988), 17.

his corporate church.[8] Historically, the accepted canon consisted of 66 books—39 Old Testament books (Genesis to Malachi) and 27 New Testament books (Matthew to Revelation).

However, during the Reformation, the Roman Catholic Church asserted that there were additional books inspired by God which belonged in the canon. What came to be known as the *Apocrypha* consisted of the books of Tobit, Judith, the Additions to Esther, the Additions to Daniel, the Wisdom of Solomon, Ecclesiasticus (also called Sirach), Baruch, the Letter of Jeremiah, and 1 and 2 Maccabees. In response to the Reformers' claims that many of the Catholic Church's practices were unbiblical, the Council of Trent (1545–1563) canonized the Apocrypha, thus deeming it to be the inspired and authoritative Word of God. This was no doubt an attempt to legitimize things like prayers for the dead (2 Macc. 12:40-46), atonement by works (Sir. 3:30), and the Immaculate Conception of Mary (Wis. 8:19-20). But after 1,500 years of being absent from the canon, did the Apocrypha suddenly deserve to be included? Certainly not.

Contrary to the teaching of the Roman Catholic Church, the canon of Scripture was not decided by Popes and councils. Rather, it was 'determined by God and discovered by man.'[9] Even as early as A.D. 68, the apostle Peter notes that Paul's writings stand alongside 'the rest of the Scriptures' (2 Pet. 3:16), indicating an acknowledgement of an accepted canon (see also 1 Tim. 5:18). And while it took some time for the church to stand together on what they recognized as being Scripture, the Council of Laodicea (A.D. 363),[10] Athanasius of Alexandria (A.D. 367), and the Third Council of Carthage (A.D. 397) acknowledged the sixty-six books of the canon, as we do today.

---

8. Michael J. Kruger, *The Question of Canon: Challenging the Status Quo in the New Testament Debate* (Downers Grove: InterVarsity Press, 2013), 40.

9. Mike Gendron, *Preparing for Eternity: Do we trust God's Word or religious traditions?* (Plano: PTG, 2011), 14.

10. With the exception of Revelation.

The Apocrypha, on the other hand, is not quoted or referred to in either the Old or New Testaments. Jesus and the Apostles never made reference to it. Many of the church fathers, as well as Palestinian Jews, rejected it. Further, the Apocrypha contains historical errors. Above all, however, there are doctrines and practices that directly contradict the teaching of the rest of Scripture! In short, the Apocrypha cannot be listed as belonging in the canon because it is not inspired by God.

But the sixty-six books of the Bible are inspired by God – 'breathed out'; they are the very Word of God.

The Issue of Inerrancy

The Apostle Paul wrote, 'Let God be found true, though every man be found a liar' (Rom. 3:4 NASB). God is a God of truth (Isa. 65:16; Jer. 10:10; John 17:3; 1 John 5:20), and He cannot lie (Num. 23:19; Titus 1:2; Heb. 6:18). Since God is true, His revealed Word to us is true, as it reflects the truthfulness of His divine character. In His high priestly prayer, the Lord Jesus entreated the Father, saying, 'Sanctify them in the truth; Your word is truth' (John 17:17).

The *inerrancy* of Scripture means that the Scriptures are true in all that they claim, and are without error. And while it has been pointed out that there have been human mistakes in the process of transmission of the Bible, we affirm that no such errors exist in the original manuscripts—those written down by those who were 'carried along by the Holy Spirit.' In fact, would that the Scriptures be found to err in even the smallest detail, we would have to question the character of the Author—would God inspire error? Surely, the Holy Spirit did not 'carry men along' into error, as that would be the height of deception; not the mark of the truthfulness of the Lord. John Frame reasons that inerrancy is 'the quality of being without error, whether caused by ignorance or deceit. Since God cannot deceive or be ignorant, God is inerrant in what he thinks and what he says. Given that Scripture is his Word, Scripture, too, is inerrant.'[11]

But, let's move on to the main issue, the issue of *authority*.

The Issue of Authority

The heart of the battle over *sola Scriptura* is a battle over the issue of authority. *Who has the right to tell people what to believe and what to do?* If the Bible is inspired by God, and thereby, inerrant, then it is also authoritative. In other words, the revealed commands of God in Scripture are binding on the believer. When Scripture speaks, God speaks.

However, during the medieval period, the Catholic Church raised 'Tradition' to a place of equal authority with Scripture. Terry Johnson writes:

> 'Tradition' included a host of extra-biblical practices and beliefs which had been received into the church over centuries, whether by common acceptance or by the decisions of Popes and councils. 'Holy writ' and 'Holy tradition' were both accepted as authoritative sources of divine truth. Over both stood the church's magisterium, its infallible teaching office, to which belongs final authority in interpreting both tradition and Scripture.[12]

Even today, the *Catechism of the Catholic Church*[13] notes, 'the Church, to whom the transmission and interpretation of Revelation is entrusted, "does not derive her certainty about all revealed truths from the holy Scriptures alone. Both Scripture and Tradition must

---

11. John M. Frame, 'Foundations of Biblical Inerrancy: Definition and Prolegomena,' in *The Inerrant Word: Biblical, Historical, Theological, and Pastoral Perspectives*, ed. John MacArthur (Wheaton: Crossway, 2016), 186.

12. Terry L. Johnson, *The Case for Traditional Protestantism: The Solas of the Reformation* (Edinburgh: Banner of Truth Trust, 2004), 20-21.

13. *Catechism of the Catholic Church*. (New York: Doubleday, 1995). From this point forward, references will be according to section numbers, rather than page numbers.

be accepted and honored with equal sentiments of devotion and reverence'" (§82). Not only is this a denial of the principle of *sola Scriptura*, it is a rejection of the inherent authority of the Word of God. Further, it is claimed that 'the task of interpreting the Word of God authentically has been entrusted solely to the Magisterium of the Church, that is, to the Pope and the bishops in communion with him' (§100). Therefore, according to the essential documents of the Roman Catholic Church, the elite spiritual hierarchy in Rome is uniquely vested with sole authority to create, institute, and mandate all religious belief and practice for every Christian in the world.

In 1870, at the First Vatican Council, it was decreed that when the Pope speaks *ex cathedra* ('from his chair'), he is speaking on behalf of God, and thereby, his words are infallible. And so, today, not only is the Magisterium of the Catholic Church deemed to be authoritative in all matters of faith and practice, but the Pope himself wields the power and authority of God when he is speaking *ex cathedra*.

But, what have they done with this self-given authority?

Changed Existing Doctrine and Practice
Of the countless changes made through the centuries, the Magisterium has seen fit to reinterpret the doctrine of justification[14] and the definition of 'grace,' increase the number of sacraments from two (Lord's Supper, Matt. 26:26-29; 1 Cor. 11:23-29; and baptism, Matt. 28:19; Acts 2:38) to seven, and even alter the nature and meaning of the Lord's Supper. In fact, on nearly every point of doctrine and practice, the Magisterium of the Roman Catholic Church has made substantial alterations away from traditional orthodoxy.

Added New Doctrine
In addition to changing doctrine and practice, the Magisterium has added numerous doctrines not found in Scripture. These

---

14. Council of Trent, Sixth Session, Canon 9.

include the Immaculate Conception, Assumption, and Mediatorial Office of Mary (§491, 966, 969), papal infallibility (§890), purgatory (§1030), baptismal regeneration (§1213), the creation of the Mass (§1367, 1377), transubstantiation (§1413), indulgences (§1471-1479), the mandated celibacy of the clergy (§1579), and countless others.

Removal of the Second Commandment

As if the alteration and addition of doctrine were not enough, the Magisterium has also removed portions of Scripture. According to the *Catechism*, the Roman Catholic Church has taken the bold step of removing the Second of the Ten Commandments (§2142). This is the commandment against idolatry first listed in Exodus 20:4, and reaffirmed nine times throughout the rest of Scripture (cf. Exod. 20:23; 34:17; Lev. 19:4; 26:1; Deut. 4:23; 5:8; 1 Cor. 10:7, 14; 1 John 5:21). However, in order to maintain the appearance of the Ten Commandments, the last commandment has been split in two, effectively functioning as numbers 9 and 10. And now, the divine command that prohibits the worshiping of carved images has been removed, and the regular practice of the veneration of images and statues is mandated and widely practiced (§1161).

But the question must be asked, by what authority has the Magisterium claimed ultimate authority?

The Supposed Apostolic Succession of Popes

According to the *Catechism*, the Lord Jesus entrusted Peter with the unique mission of being the universal leader of the church. Citing Matthew 16:18, it asserts that 'because of the faith he confessed Peter will remain the unshakeable rock of the Church' (§552). Further, Peter is believed to have been entrusted with 'a specific authority'— 'the keys of the kingdom of heaven'—which is nothing short of the 'authority to govern the house of God, which is the Church' (§553). Based primarily on this text, it is believed that Peter was commissioned by Christ to be the very first Pope, thus beginning a line of papal succession which has continued even until today.

However, rightly understood, Matthew 16 is not about Christ granting to Peter the authority over the church; it's about *Christ* declaring *His* intention to build the church! And the 'rock' on which Christ builds is not Peter himself, but rather, his earlier confession of faith in Jesus (v. 16): 'You are the Christ, the Son of the living God!' Commenting on this verse, John Calvin writes:

> From this it appears how the name Peter belongs both to Peter and to other believers; that is, founded on the faith of Christ they are fitted by a holy concord into the spiritual building, so that God may dwell in their midst. For since Christ here declares that this is the common foundation of the whole Church, He wishes to join with Peter all the believers who are going to exist in the world. It is as if He said, 'You are now just a tiny number of men, and therefore your confession has little worth at present; but the time will soon come when it will stand out splendidly and will spread far wider.' And this availed not a little to encourage the disciples to constancy; because, although their faith was obscure and lowly, yet they were chosen by the Lord as first fruits so that at last from this insignificant beginning there should arise the new Church which would stand triumphant against all the designs of hell.[15]

While it's true that Peter's name (*petros*) means 'rock' in Greek, the issue is over the meaning of Peter's being the 'rock.' Is this a prooftext for the act of Jesus passing the baton of authority to Peter as the first Pope? Furthermore, *is Peter the rock on which the church is built?*

Ephesians 2:20 teaches that the church is 'built on the foundation of the apostles and prophets, Christ Jesus Himself being the cornerstone.' Elsewhere, Christ is called 'the stone which the

---

15. *Calvin's Commentaries: A Harmony of the Gospels—Matthew, Mark and Luke*, trans. T.H.L. Parker, eds. David W. Torrance & Thomas F. Torrance (Grand Rapids: Eerdmans, 1972), 186.

builders have rejected' which has 'become the chief cornerstone' (Ps. 118:22; cf. Matt. 21:42; Mark 12:10; Luke 20:17; Acts 4:11). The apostle Paul wrote, 'for no one can lay a foundation other than that which is laid, which is Jesus Christ' (1 Cor. 3:11). Further, he asserts that even during their wilderness wandering, the Israelites 'drank from the spiritual Rock that followed them, and the Rock was Christ' (1 Cor. 10:4). Even Peter himself taught that Jesus Christ was the 'the cornerstone' (1 Pet. 2:4, 6-7); and Christians are 'living stones ... being built up as a spiritual house' (v. 5); they are built squarely on Christ.

Jesus did not announce or intend that Peter would be the first Pope, nor did He impart to him any kind of authority as Head of the church—Christ Himself 'is the head of the body, the church' (Col. 1:18). And the 'keys of the kingdom' were given collectively to the church, to be exercised under the spiritual authority of Christ's true vicar—the Holy Spirit (John 14:16-17; 16:5-15). Neither the Pope nor the Magisterium has the authority to speak for God; only the Holy Spirit speaking through His living word (Heb. 4:12). And so, recognizing the inherent authority of the Word of God, we must affirm *sola Scriptura*. John Calvin writes, 'our conviction of the truth of Scripture must be derived from a higher source than human conjectures, judgments, or reasons; namely, the secret testimony of the Spirit.'[16]

Rome has no true power; the emperor has no clothes. Rather, Scripture is vested with the full authority of Jesus Christ, as it is His revealed word. And if the Word of God is *inspired*, *inerrant*, and *authoritative*, then we must also concede that it is altogether *sufficient*.

The Issue of Sufficiency

It is important to note that 'the Reformers believed in *sola Scriptura*, not *solo*, that is, Scripture *alone*, not Scripture *only*, not Scripture

---

16. John Calvin, *Institutes of the Christian Religion*, trans. Henry Beveridge (1559; reprint, Peabody: Hendrickson, 2008), 33.

in isolation from the church and its history.'[17] There is a place for creeds, councils, and traditions. In fact, the illumination of the Holy Spirit has carried along countless believers in history into a greater understanding of the Word of God. *Creeds* are simply affirmations of biblical truth. Many *councils* have been comprised of godly church leaders who have labored together for better understanding and for the discovery of doctrine. And *traditions* are oftentimes the best practices of Christian believers who desire to honor Christ.

However, the danger comes when the traditions of men assault the authority of the Word of God. This was the reason for Jesus' rebuke of the Pharisees in Matthew 15, when they asked Him why His disciples violated the tradition of the elders. He responded, 'And why do you break the commandment of God for the sake of your tradition?' (v. 3). Because for years, they had been burdening believers with the yoke of legalistic religion, and placing their traditions above God's revealed commands. So, Jesus rebuked them, saying:

> You hypocrites! Well did Isaiah prophesy of you, when he said: 'This people honors me with their lips, but their heart is far from me; in vain do they worship me, teaching as doctrines the commandments of men' (vv. 7-9).

Even Paul warned the church to 'see to it that no one takes you captive by philosophy and empty deceit, according to human tradition, according to the elementary spirits of the world, and not according to Christ' (Col. 2:8). Again, tradition is fine, but not when it supersedes the Word of God, and takes captive the believer. No, we are 'not to go beyond what is written' (1 Cor. 4:6). John warns, 'if anyone adds to [the revelation of Scripture], God will add to him the plagues described in [the Bible]' (Rev. 22:18). Scripture alone is our authority—not traditions, not councils, not denominations, not Popes, not even the angels in heaven (cf. Gal. 1:8).

---

17. Johnson, *The Case for Traditional Protestantism*, 35.

The Lord Jesus claims for Himself all authority in heaven and on earth (Matt. 28:18; cf. Matt. 11:27; John 3:35; 5:22–24; 17:2; 19:11; etc.), and He has given us His Spirit, who has given us His Word. And it is *sufficient* for us. W. Robert Godfrey writes, 'The Protestant position ... is that all things *necessary* for salvation and concerning faith and life are taught in the Bible with enough clarity that the ordinary believer can find them there and understand.'[18]

James R. White writes:

> The Bible claims to be the *sole and sufficient* infallible rule of faith for the Christian church. The Scriptures are not in need of any supplement; their authority comes from their nature as God-breathed revelation; their authority is *not* dependent upon man, church, or council. The Scriptures are self-consistent, self-interpreting, and self-authenticating. The Christian church looks to the Scriptures as the only infallible and sufficient rule of faith, and the church is always subject to the Word, and is constantly reformed thereby.[19]

At the risk of driving too many nails into the door, consider what Matthew Barrett writes: '*Sola Scriptura* means that *only Scripture, because it is God's inspired Word, is our inerrant, sufficient, and final authority for the church.*'[20]

How did the Roman Catholic Church respond to the Protestant declaration of *sola Scriptura*? In 1559, Pope Pius IV said:

> Since experience teaches that, if the reading of the Holy Bible in the vernacular is permitted generally without discrimination, more damage than advantage will result because of the boldness

18. W. Robert Godfrey, 'What Do We Mean By Sola Scriptura?' in *Sola Scriptura: The Protestant Position on the Bible*, ed. Don Kistler (Orlando: Reformation Trust, 2009), 2.

19. James R. White, *Scripture Alone: Exploring the Bible's Accuracy, Authority, and Authenticity* (Minneapolis: Bethany House, 2004), 28.

20. Matthew Barrett, *God's Word Alone: The Authority of Scripture* (Grand Rapids: Zondervan, 2016), 23.

of men, the judgment of the bishops and inquisitors is to serve as a guide in this regard.[21]

And with that, Rome banned all Bible translations except the Latin Vulgate, placing them on a list of 'forbidden books.' The Pope added, 'Whoever reads or has such a translation in his possession without ... permission cannot be absolved from his sins until he has turned in these Bibles.'[22] This was nothing less than an attempt to wrestle authority away from the Word of God, and confer it on the Magisterium.

John Rogers, the first English martyr, was a disciple of William Tyndale. And before being burned at the stake, he was interrogated by one of the bishops, who maintained, 'You can prove nothing by the Scripture,' he said. 'The Scripture is dead; it must have a living expositor,' no doubt referring to the office of the Pope. But Rogers replied, 'No, the Scripture is alive!'[23]

Rogers was right.

We have a living God who speaks to us presently through His Word. And through the word of truth—the gospel of our salvation, we are saved and sanctified; our conscience held captive to the Word of God.

We affirm:

All Scripture is breathed out by God and profitable for teaching, for reproof, for correction, and for training in righteousness, that the man of God may be complete, equipped for every good work (2 Tim. 3:16-17).

---

21. W. Robert Godfrey, 'What Do We Mean By Sola Scriptura?' in *Sola Scriptura: The Protestant Position on the Bible*, ed. Don Kistler (Orlando: Reformation Trust, 2009), 9.

22. ibid.

23. Timothy George, *Theology of the Reformers* (Nashville: B&H, 2013), 341.

For the grace of God has appeared, bringing salvation ...
(Titus 2:11)

3.
Sola Gratia
(Grace Alone)

In his introduction to John Owen's classic work, *The Death of Death in the Death of Christ*, J.I. Packer writes that 'there is really only *one* point to be made in the field of soteriology: the point that *God saves sinners*.'[1] The Word of God affirms that 'salvation is from the Lord' (Ps. 37:39; Jon. 2:9 NASB). It originates with Him, and is given freely as a gift. This is what is known as *grace*. Grace is *unmerited favor*. Much like with a birthday present, no one spends all year working to earn it, neither does a believer work to earn the grace of God. And the Reformers came to believe that a proper understanding of the grace of God in salvation was vital to the Christian faith. Luther called the issue 'the hinge on which all turns.'[2] It is the issue of *sola gratia*, or 'grace alone.'

When Martin Luther was first beginning his doctoral studies at Wittenberg, Peter Lombard's twelfth-century theological textbook *Four Books of Sentences* was required reading. However, it was Lombard's references to Augustine that drew Luther's eye. At a time when the young Luther was still battling his own demons, it

---

1. John Owen, *The Death of Death in the Death of Christ* (1684; reprint, Edinburgh: Banner of Truth Trust, 1959), 6.

2. Martin Luther, *The Bondage of the Will*, trans. J.I. Packer and O.R. Johnson (1525; reprint, London: James Clark & Co. Ltd., 1957), 319.

was the issues of sin and the human condition that would trouble him the most. But Augustine would help him wrestle through the issues, and ultimately, lead him to the apostle Paul.[3]

Augustine and the Human Condition

Aurelius Augustine was born in North Africa in A.D. 354 to a Christian mother and a pagan father. Despite his mother's desperate prayers for his conversion, Augustine plunged himself headlong into a life of sin. Satisfying his appetites proved elusive for him, as he began searching for truth. This ultimately led him to Milan, where he would study philosophy. He dabbled in the Bible, but did not find it all too interesting. He soon found himself in the charge of Ambrose, the bishop of Milan, who would teach him the Scriptures. Soon, while sitting under the preaching of Ambrose, Augustine became convicted of his own sinfulness, but wasn't sure what to do about it. B.K. Kuiper records what happened next:

> He rushed out into the little garden behind the house. The copy of Paul's epistles which he was carrying he laid on the bench beside him. His soul was profoundly agitated. He got up from the bench and flung himself down on the grass beneath a fig tree. As he was lying there he heard a child next door sing the ditty: *Tolle, lege; tolle, lege,* which means, 'Take up and read; take up and read.' He got up, returned to the bench, picked up the copy of Paul's epistles, and read: 'Let us behave decently, as in the daytime, not in orgies and drunkenness, not in sexual immorality and debauchery, not in dissension and jealousy. Rather, clothe yourselves with the Lord Jesus Christ, and do not think about how to gratify the desires of the sinful nature' (Rom. 13:13-14).[4]

Augustine was cut to the heart, so he repented of his sins—many of the same ones listed in Paul's epistle—and believed on the Lord

---

3.   Stephen J. Nichols, *Martin Luther: A Guided Tour of His Life and Thought* (Phillipsburg: Presbyterian & Reformed, 2002), 31.

4.   B.K. Kuiper, *The Church in History* (1951; Grand Rapids: Eerdmans, 1996), 37.

Jesus Christ, and was converted. Soon after, in 386, Augustine pursued his studies under Ambrose, and would eventually become the bishop of Hippo, in his native country of North Africa. He would preach and teach, found a monastery, and publish many books. But it is his spiritual biography, *Confessions* (c. 400), for which he is best known.

Augustine's *Confessions* recounts the story of his life and conversion, focusing specifically on his past sins and the grace of God to save him. In the opening sections, he chronicles the workings of his own restless heart, as he contemplates his life of sin. One incident in particular stands out; Augustine describes a time where he steals some pears from his neighbor. He describes how he stole them, not because he was hungry or even needed them, but simply because he wanted to steal. He writes, 'I lusted to thieve,' and even though 'it was foul,' he says, 'I loved it.'[5]

But in the midst of his admission of guilt, he lamented over his own sin, realizing that it was a terrible offense to God. Furthermore, he realized that he was not simply *committing sins*, but that *he himself was sinful*. It was his nature, not just to commit acts of sin, but to love the sin itself. Carl Trueman writes, 'The picture Augustine paints in the *Confessions* is stark and disturbing. Sin is a pervasive power that controls and defines human beings. It is something that dominates personal existence and offers no means of escape.'[6] In the throes of his anguish, Augustine, channeling the apostle Paul in Romans 7, writes:

> I, convicted by the truth, had nothing at all to answer ... in vain I 'delighted in Thy law according to the inner man,' when 'another law in my members rebelled against the law of my mind, and

---

5. Augustine, *Confessions* 2.4. Translated by Edward Bouverie Pusey. (Chicago: William Benton, 1952).

6. Carl Trueman, *Grace Alone: Salvation as a Gift of God* (Grand Rapids: Zondervan, 2017), 61.
    I am indebted to Dr. Trueman for pointing to the connection between Augustine and Luther.

led me captive under the law of sin which was in my members.' For the law of sin is the violence of custom, whereby the mind is drawn and holden, even against its will; but deservedly, for that it willingly fell into it. 'Who then should deliver me thus wretched from the body of this death,' but Thy grace only, through Jesus Christ our Lord?[7]

In his *Confessions*, Augustine acknowledges the truth of Scripture regarding the nature of fallen man, destroyed by sin. Even the apostle Paul calls himself a 'wretched man' (Rom. 7:24) who is in need of redemption from his body of death. The weight of biblical evidence, compounded with his own personal experiences with sin, led Augustine to understand and believe in the doctrine of *original sin*, or the *total depravity of man*. And he would come to see that the only possible way of salvation was by the grace of God. In his work, *On Admonition and Grace*, Augustine writes, 'The grace of God through Jesus Christ our Lord must be understood as that by which *alone* men are delivered from evil, and without which they do absolutely no good thing, whether in thought, or will and affection, or in deed.'[8]

This concept of God's *grace alone* being the only way of salvation would be the key element in Martin Luther's new understanding.

Luther's *Bondage of the Will*

By the 1520s, Luther was already waist-deep in many of his doctrinal beliefs, namely the belief that salvation was 'by grace alone'— although he admits, 'I didn't learn my theology all at once, I had to ponder over it even more deeply, and my spiritual trials were of help to me in this.'[9] Luther, no doubt identifying with Augustine and Paul in their lamentations over sin, was fully convinced of his

---

7.   Augustine, *Confessions* 8.5.

8.   Vernon J. Bourke, ed. *The Essential Augustine* (Indianapolis: Hackett Publishing Co., 1981), 176. Emphasis added.

9.   Nichols, *Martin Luther*, 71.

own depravity, and knew that it was only by the grace of God he was redeemed.

Further, he knew that not even the Pope had the power to grant him the forgiveness he so desperately needed, and had stated as much in his Ninety-Five Theses. Elsewhere, he wrote, 'If the Pope does have the power to release anyone from purgatory, why in the name of love does he not abolish purgatory by letting everyone out?'[10] And the reason the Pope didn't empty purgatory was because he couldn't. In fact, no act of man can spring a soul from divine punishment and into the saving arms of God—not by 'the will of the flesh, nor of the will of man, but [only] of God' (John 1:12).

But Rome held to an adapted view of *Pelagianism*—a denial of original sin, and the belief that the human will is able to choose to do good on its own; further, that salvation was 'a reward for good works freely performed by human beings.'[11] Having read Augustine, Luther would have no doubt been familiar with the issues surrounding this teaching, as Pelagius (A.D. 360-418) was an opponent of Augustine. In fact, the two scholars warred fiercely over the doctrines of sin, predestination, and the human will. Eventually, Pelagius was condemned as a heretic by the Council of Carthage in 418.

However, the Roman Catholic Church had since modified its view of sin and the human will, adopting a form of *Semi-Pelagianism*—the belief that humans participate in their salvation; in effect, they choose to be saved, and subsequently, grow by the infused grace of God. Luther had been vocal in his opposition to this view, debating against it often. However, in response to Luther, the humanist scholar Erasmus—formerly his Reformation ally—set out to disprove Luther's view, boldly declaring the triumph of the human will.

---

10. Roland H. Bainton, *Here I Stand: A Life of Martin Luther* (Peabody: Hendrickson, 1950), 64.

11. Timothy George, *Theology of the Reformers* (Nashville: B&H, 2013), 74.

Erasmus vs. Luther

In September 1524, under pressure from the Catholic Church, Erasmus penned an attack on Luther's theology, titled *Diatribe Concerning Free-Will*. In his work he maintains that the Fall, although negatively impacting the human will, did not destroy it. At the heart of Erasmus' argument is the belief that human beings, although weakened by sin, are able to perform good deeds by their own free-will, which includes their ability to cooperate *with* God to achieve their salvation. While he does not deny outright the sovereignty of God and the need for grace, Erasmus did nothing more than echo the *de facto* arguments of the Catholic Church's Semi-Pelagian position. Rome hailed the *Diatribe* as a theological victory, believing that it had dealt a death blow to Luther's arguments. But Luther's response would rock the Church in a way they never could have imagined.

In December 1525, a response finally came. Seizing on Erasmus' title, Luther offered what has been called 'the greatest piece of writing that came from [his] pen'—*The Bondage of the Will*. J.I. Packer notes, 'the Luther whom we meet in *The Bondage of the Will* is not Luther the pamphleteer, nor Luther the (largely extempore) preacher, but Dr. Luther, the systematic theologian—and one of a high order.'[12] Luther, he adds, is 'a great-hearted warrior; a thorough exegete (he wins the battle of the texts hands down); a profound systematic theologian; and above all, an unflinching defender of the grace of a sovereign God.'[13]

After first establishing the authority and clarity of Scripture, Luther takes Erasmus to task point by point, bringing the Word of God to bear on every theological assertion. And, frankly, he's relentless. Not only does Luther attack his main arguments, but he also picks apart his supporting details, even calling Erasmus out on

---

12. From the Introduction to *Bondage of the Will*, eds. J.I. Packer and O.R. Johnson (1525; London: James Clark & Co. Ltd., 1957), 45.

13. ibid., 47.

his sloppiness with his citations.[14] But, it is on Erasmus' assertion regarding man's ability to do good that Luther sets his sights.

Luther appeals to Scripture, namely the first few chapters of Romans, to showcase the doctrine of *human depravity*. Perhaps the most damning passage regarding human ability comes at the conclusion of Paul's diatribe against self-righteousness in Romans 3. The apostle Paul, weaving a litany of Old Testament texts, writes:

> There is none righteous, not even one;
> There is none who understands, there is none who seeks for God;
> All have turned aside, together they have become useless;
> There is none who does good, there is not even one.
> Their throat is an open grave, with their tongues they keep deceiving,
> The poison of asps is under their lips;
> Whose mouth is full of cursing and bitterness;
> Their feet are swift to shed blood,
> Destruction and misery are in their paths,
> And the path of peace they have not known.
> There is no fear of God before their eyes (Rom. 3:10-18 NASB).

Commenting on these verses, Luther writes, 'I am astounded that, when Paul so often uses these comprehensive terms, 'all,' 'none,' 'not,' 'never,' 'without,' ... I am amazed [at] how it has happened that in the face of these comprehensive terms and statements, others that are contrary, yes, contradictory to them should have won acceptance.'[15] In other words, when Paul says, '*none* are righteous,' how could anyone walk away with the notion that *anyone* could be capable of meriting righteousness. When Paul says, '*no one* seeks after God, how could anyone conclude that it were possible for *anyone* to seek God by their own human will? Luther then says that

---

14. Luther, *Bondage of the Will*, 73.
15. ibid., 298.

the only way you could arrive at such a conclusion is if you were 'to introduce a new grammar, and a new mode of speech!'[16]

Furthermore, if we understand the Scriptures rightly alongside Augustine and Luther, we see that we are 'dead in our trespasses and sins' (Eph. 2:1, 5), 'slaves of sin' (Rom. 6:6, 12, 20; cf. John 8:34), 'loving the darkness; hating the light' (John 3:19), 'enemies of God' (Rom. 5:10), 'hostile to God' (Rom. 8:7), and thereby, 'children of wrath' (Eph. 2:3). Jeremiah 17:9 says that man's heart is 'deceitful and desperately wicked.' And David writes that he was 'brought forth in iniquity ... conceived in sin' (Ps. 51:5). In other words, born that way! And in our fallen, fleshly condition, according to Romans 8:8, we cannot please God because we are 'not even *able* to do so.' The only logical conclusion that we can draw from the biblical evidence is that, apart from the grace of God, the soul is dead.

And if the soul is dead, the will is dead.

The Myth of Free-Will
In fact, in light of Scripture, it becomes clear that there *is* no such thing as 'free-will.' According to Romans 6, human beings are either 'slaves of sin' (vv. 13, 16-17, 20) or 'slaves of righteousness' (vv. 18, 22). There's no neutral category. Jesus said, 'No one can serve two masters, for either he will hate the one and love the other, or he will be devoted to the one and despise the other' (Matt. 6:24). Luther adds, 'Hence it follows that 'free-will' without God's grace is not free at all, but is the permanent prisoner and bondslave of evil, since it cannot turn itself to good.'[17] In other words, fallen humanity lacks the ability to make spiritual decisions or accomplish righteous acts. Isaiah records that our deeds done in unrighteousness are but 'filthy rags' to God (Isa. 64:6). Every righteous thing we think we're doing ends up being nothing more than an exercise in self-righteousness. Luther concludes, 'It follows, therefore, that "free-will" is obviously

---

16. ibid., 299.

17. ibid., 104.

a term applicable only to the Divine Majesty; for only He can do, and does (as the Psalmist sings) 'whatever he wills in heaven and earth' (Ps. 135.6).'[18]

Therefore, the only way a sinner can be saved is if God chooses to do so—*God saves sinners*. As believers, we affirm that the Lord God is sovereign (Exod. 33:19; Ps. 115:3; Rom. 8:28-30), all-powerful (Job 42:1-2; Col. 1:7; Heb. 1:3), all-knowing (Ps. 139:2-6; 147:5; Heb. 4:13), and righteous (Ps. 48:10; 119:137, 142; Jer. 12:1; John 17:25). No one can understand His ways or His will (Isa. 55:8-9), yet we willingly submit to it. In fact, Jesus taught the disciples to pray, 'Your kingdom come, *Your will be done*' (Matt. 6:10, emphasis added). And if human beings are altogether dead in sin and unable to save themselves from judgment, then only God, according to His sovereign will, can reach down from heaven, extend His hand, and pull sinners out of the grave (like Lazarus!). And He does it because He chooses to do it. Jesus said, 'No one can come to me unless the Father who sent me draws him. And I will raise him up on the last day' (John 6:44). Paul writes, 'But *by His doing* you are in Christ Jesus, who became to us wisdom from God, and righteousness and sanctification, and redemption, that, just as it is written, "Let him who boasts, boast in the Lord."' (1 Cor. 1:30-31, emphasis added).

We routinely appeal to the grace of God, the mercy of God, and the sovereignty of God in all things. We consistently rely on God to uphold creation, order events, set up and take down leaders, and influence governments. We humbly submit to God in all His knowledge, wisdom, goodness, and righteousness. We trust Him to make provision, to bless, to curse, to heal, and to work reconciliation. We even pray to God for salvation for others—our unsaved friends and family. We yield to His sovereign will at *every* point; yet we so desperately want to cling to the notion that *we* exercised *our* own free will to be saved or that *we* gave spiritual rebirth to ourselves!?

---

18. ibid., 105.

Oh, that we might behold the pure grace of God in salvation—our hearts would melt in adoration and thanksgiving! Our pride would be smashed, our strength would fail, our knees would buckle, and we would fall down and worship the Lord! That's why we're exhorted, not to pull ourselves up by our bootstraps, but to 'draw near to the throne of grace' (Heb. 4:16).

But people say, 'That's not fair!' or 'I don't like that God chooses who will be saved'—as if it impugns the character of God. Erasmus used to say, 'Let God be good.' But Luther replied, 'Let God be God!' This doctrine is not from men, otherwise we could mutiny against it. Rather, it's from the Lord. For He says in Exodus 33:19, 'I will have mercy on whom I have mercy, and I will have compassion on whom I have compassion' (NIV). And Paul fields the question in Romans 9, 'What shall we say then? There is no injustice with God, is there? May it never be!' (v. 14). 'It does not depend on the man who *wills* or the man who runs, but on God who has mercy' (v. 16, emphasis added). Paul continues the argument:

> You will say to me then, 'Why does He still find fault? For who resists His will?' On the contrary, who are you, O man, who answers back to God? The thing molded will not say to the molder, 'Why did you make me like this,' will it? Or does not the potter have a right over the clay to make from the same lump one vessel for honorable use, and another for common use? (Rom. 9:19-21 NASB).

In our self-reliance and stubbornness and pride, we stand defiant against the sovereign will of God, but we stand in error. This is the same God who speaks worlds into existence (Gen. 1:1ff), turns back the sundial (2 Kings 20:11), calms oceans (Mark 4:39) and divides the seas (Exod. 14:21), and raises the dead (Mark 5:21-43; John 11:39-44), and laughs at rebellious nations (Ps. 2:4). And this same God opposes the proud ... but gives grace to those who are humble (Prov. 3:34; Jas. 4:6; 1 Pet. 5:5). Luther writes:

'But a man cannot be thoroughly humbled till he realises that his salvation is utterly beyond his own powers, counsels, efforts, will and works, and depends absolutely on the will, counsel, pleasure and work of Another—God alone.'[19]

Therefore, he writes:

'It is, then, fundamentally necessary and wholesome for Christians to know that God foreknows nothing contingently, but that He foresees, purposes, and does all things according to His own immutable, eternal and infallible will.'[20]

The exercise of God's divine will is not merely an arbitrary thing. God is not passive or nonchalant in His decision. Nor is He unjust, malicious, or vindictive. No, Scripture teaches that God's kindness and goodness toward human beings is an extension of His grace, and it is nothing short of amazing.

But how does a believer receive His grace? This was a major point of contention with the Reformers.

The Means of Grace

In Luther's day (and today), Rome taught that salvation came by the grace of God, but their understanding of 'grace' was markedly different than what the Bible teaches. For the Roman Catholic Church, *grace* was a 'thing'—a force of divine power bestowed on believers to accomplish spiritual tasks. A shot in the arm, a boost; one writer even likened it to a spiritual Red Bull.[21] At the behest of the Pope, this 'grace would be given to those who wanted and pursued it, and it saved only insofar as it *enabled* people to become holy and so win their salvation.'[22] And so, Roman Catholicism is

---

19. ibid., 100.

20. ibid., 80.

21. Michael Reeves & Tim Chester, *Why the Reformation Still Matters* (Wheaton: Crossway, 2016), 88.

22. ibid., 83.

built on the notion of obtaining this spiritual substance they call 'grace.' And the way to obtain the grace of God was through various 'means of grace' known as *sacraments*.

The word 'sacrament' comes from the Latin word *sacramentum*, which means 'sacred oath' but later used to speak of a mysterious means by which God imparts His grace. In Roman Catholicism, there are seven sacraments. They are as follows:

- *Baptism* cleanses from original sin, provides spiritual rebirth or regeneration, and begins the process of justification (§694, 1213, 1250).
- *Confirmation* bestows the Holy Spirit, leading to increased spiritual power and sealing to the Catholic Church.
- *Penance* removes the penalty of sins committed after baptism and confirmation.
- *Holy Eucharist* is where Christ is re-offered up as a non-bloody sacrifice, and the benefits of Calvary are perpetuated and applied to the life of the believer (§1367, 1377, 1382).
- *Marriage* provides a special grace bestowed on couples who choose to wed in the Catholic Church.
- *Anointing the sick* bestows grace on those who are sick, old, or near death.
- *Holy orders* confer special grace and spiritual power upon the leadership of the Church (bishops, priests, deacons) as representatives of Christ.

It is believed that the sacraments function *ex opere operato*—'from the work worked.' In other words, they have intrinsic spiritual powers that works on their own, independently of the faith of the person receiving them. Simply put, grace is received through the sacraments themselves. However, this phenomenon is purely man-made, and is taught nowhere in Scripture.

The Reformers believed that 'the place of growing in grace was tied to the ongoing practice of certain means of grace: the reading and preaching of the Word and the right administration of the sacraments.'[23] Further, the sacraments to be administered were those explicitly commanded by Christ, namely *baptism* and *the Lord's Supper*. But they did not understand them the same way the Catholic Church did; for baptism does not cleanse from sin or produce regeneration, rather, it is a *sign* of faith. And the Lord's Supper does not consist of ingesting the literal body and blood of Jesus Christ; it is a spiritual reality.

The grace of God cannot be transacted like a commodity; it cannot be handled like an object. It cannot be bought or sold, worked for or earned. Instead, it must be freely given by God Himself.

God's Grace

If *grace* is unmerited favor; the kindness and goodness of God extended to those who are undeserving, then it must be given directly by Him in the ways in which He chooses to dispense it. In the Bible, we see the grace of God manifested in the person of Jesus Christ, whereby He gives us *Himself*: 'For the grace of God has appeared, bringing salvation for all people' (Titus 2:11). The grace of God comes through the love of God—'For God so loved the world He gave His only begotten Son' (John 3:16). He's given to us according to His own will, not according to the will of sinful men. For Romans 5:8 says that even *'while we were yet sinners*, Christ died for us. In fact, our salvation, our justification, was 'a gift by His grace through the redemption which is in Christ Jesus' (Rom. 3:24).

Paul tells us that, in Adam all sinned; all died—'death reigned' (Rom. 5:14, 17). And even in the giving of the Law of Moses, sin and transgression only increased. More Law, more death. We were in a downward spiral, completely incapable of pulling ourselves out. But God took pity on us; He showed compassion. He sent another Adam, a perfect Adam; One who could satisfy all the Law

---

23. Michael Allen, 'Sanctification, Perseverance, and Assurance,' in ed. Matthew Barrett, *Reformation Theology: A Systematic Summary* (Wheaton: Crossway, 2017), 562.

and accomplish a perfect righteousness. So that, 'through one act of righteousness'—the cross—'there resulted justification of life to all men' (v. 18 NASB).

Even while we were dead in our trespasses, enslaved to our sin, ensnared in an ocean of wickedness, Paul says, 'grace abounded all the more, that, as sin reigned in death, even so grace might reign through righteousness to eternal life through Jesus Christ our Lord' (vv. 20-21 NASB). God saw us struggling in our blood, and He said, 'Live!' (cf. Ezek. 16:6). *He* has removed our hearts of stone and given us hearts of flesh (Ezek. 36:26). And *He* poured out 'grace upon grace' (John 1:16) through sending His Son.

How marvelous! How wonderful is the amazing grace of God!

> For by *grace* you have been saved through faith. And this is not your own doing; it is the gift of God, not as a result of works, so that no one may boast. For we are his workmanship, created in Christ Jesus for good works, which God prepared beforehand, that we should walk in them (Eph. 2:8-10).

We are saved by God's grace, and by grace alone—*sola gratia*.

For we maintain that a man is justified by faith
apart from works of the Law.
(Romans 3:28 NASB)

4.
Sola Fide
(Faith Alone)

By the year 1540, the Reformation was in full swing, as hotbeds of Protestantism were springing up all over Europe. Martin Luther, Martin Bucer, and Philip Melanchthon had led the fight in Germany for two decades, while simultaneously, Ulrich Zwingli, followed by Heinrich Bullinger, would launch the Swiss Reformation. France would see Reformation first through Guillaume Farel, followed by John Calvin and Theodore Beza. In England, it would be ignited through the labors of William Tyndale and Thomas Cranmer, but set ablaze through the witness of men like John Hooper, Hugh Latimer, and Nicholas Ridley. John Knox would bring the Reformation to Scotland, George Browne to Ireland, Menno Simmons to the Netherlands, and Johannes Bugenhagen to Denmark. In fact, during the sixteenth century, more than fifty of the eighty-five free, imperial cities within the Holy Roman Empire would become Protestant.[1]

What bound them together, however, was more than just a rejection of the errors of the Roman Catholic Church. They were bound by a commitment to the Word of God and to the gospel of the Lord Jesus Christ. As we noted earlier, it has been said that *sola Scriptura* was the *formal* principle of the Reformation, that is, at

---

1.   Timothy George, *Theology of the Reformers* (Nashville: B&H, 2013), 119.

the heart of its method, while its *material* principle—the heart of its content—was *sola fide*, or 'faith alone.' During his debate with Cardinal Sadoleto, John Calvin noted that *sola fide* was 'the first and keenest subject of controversy between us.' And if removed, he argued, 'the glory of Christ is extinguished, religion is abolished, the church destroyed, and the hope of salvation utterly overthrown.'[2] As we'll see, at the core of *sola fide* lies the doctrine of justification.

The Truth of the Gospel

In Galatians 2, the apostle Paul recounts an episode which occurred between him and the apostle Peter. He notes that 'when Cephas [Peter] came to Antioch,' Paul confronted him publicly (v. 11). But, what would cause two apostles to square off? What issue could be so dire? He notes in verse 14, that it was a critical issue; an issue pertaining to 'the truth of the gospel.' There was great confusion, and Peter was at the center of the dilemma.

A delegation of Jewish leaders had come from Jerusalem. It is believed that the delegation was made up of Judaizers—those who maintained that salvation consisted of more than simply faith in Jesus Christ, but also strict adherence to Mosaic rituals and regulations. Further, these Jewish legalists would no doubt have held onto the practice of strict separation from all non-Jews, as they had done for many years. Their arrival in Antioch caused great fear in Peter (v. 12), because he, along with other Jewish Christians, had embraced the Gentile Christians as brothers and sisters in the Lord.

In response to the arrival of the Jewish delegation, Peter began to withdraw from fellowship with the Gentiles. In fact, the majority of Jews in Antioch followed his lead, and began to separate. This effectively created the illusion of a two-class division: the Jewish Christians being the more spiritual; the Gentile Christians being less spiritual.

---

2. Quoted in Terry L. Johnson, *The Case for Traditional Protestantism: The Solas of the Reformation* (Edinburgh: Banner of Truth Trust, 2004), 76.

When Paul heard about it, he was furious. Immediately, he recognized the behavior as hypocrisy (v. 13), and took action against the ringleader, Peter. Paul notes that this self-imposed separation created confusion, as it muddied the waters with regard to the gospel. Peter was, in effect, preaching another gospel (cf. Gal. 1:8-9), and Paul confronts him 'because he stood condemned' (v. 11).

Paul poses the question, 'If you, being a Jew, live like the Gentiles and not like the Jews, how is it that you compel the Gentiles to live like Jews?' (v. 14 NASB). In other words, the Jewish Christians had been experiencing the benefits of Christian liberty, not adhering to the minutiae of the Mosaic law. Essentially, they were now living like the Gentiles. But upon the arrival of the Judaizers, Peter effectively reversed his stance, separating from the Gentiles specifically *because* they were not obeying Mosaic law. He was now placing a burden of law-keeping on them that he himself had been freed from through the redeeming work of Christ, along with the rest of the Christian fellowship. And Paul calls it like it is: hypocrisy.

He presses Peter on 'the truth of the gospel,' reminding him of the most essential truth—a truth that Peter no doubt knew very well—'that a man is not justified by the works of the Law but through faith in Christ Jesus' (v. 16 NASB). In fact, in order to emphasize his point, he restates the phrase two more times: 'even we have believed in Christ Jesus, that we may be justified by faith in Christ, and not by the works of the Law; since by the works of the Law shall no flesh be justified.' Thankfully, we know that Peter repented, and the truth of the gospel was upheld.

The notion that people are *justified by faith apart from works* is prevalent in the New Testament, but it would need to be rescued from a thousand years of obscurity, as it is the focal point of the gospel of Jesus Christ.

The Recovery of the Doctrine of Justification
It's been said that the re-discovery of the doctrine of justification took place in a tower in Wittenberg, Germany. Somewhere around

the year 1519, two years after posting his Ninety-Five Theses, Martin Luther was locked away, studying Paul's letter to the Romans. He was relentless; desperately trying to understand the phrase 'the righteousness [justice] of God' in Romans 1:17. Up to that point, he chafed under the phrase, even hating it! He saw 'the righteousness of God' as the perfect standard of God to which all sinners are held; a standard that no one can hope to accomplish. And this made Luther angry. 'Isn't it enough that we miserable sinners, lost for all eternity because of original sin, are oppressed by every kind of calamity through the Ten Commandments?' he said. 'Why does God heap sorrow upon sorrow through the Gospel and through the Gospel threaten us with his justice and his wrath?'[3] To Luther, the implications of this verse painted God out to be vindictive and merciless; a mean child holding a magnifying glass over an anthill, burning the ants under His fiery judgment, and laughing all the while.

But then something clicked.

After meditating on the words day and night, Luther arrived at a new understanding. He writes:

> I began to understand that in this verse the justice of God is that by which the person lives by a gift of God, that is by faith. I began to understand that this verse means that the justice of God is revealed through the Gospel, but it is a passive justice, i.e. that by which the merciful God justifies us by faith, as it is written: 'The just person lives by faith.' All at once I felt that I had been born again and entered into paradise itself through open gates.[4]

Suddenly, Luther no longer hated God, but rejoiced in His name! Now, he understood 'the righteousness of God' not as being active (something he had to achieve), but passive (something Christ

---

3. Quoted in Michael Reeves & Tim Chester, *Why the Reformation Still Matters* (Wheaton: Crossway, 2016), 25.

4. ibid., 26.

achieved on his behalf). Now, the chains were off, and he worshiped the Lord with all his heart. Luther confessed:

> If you have a true faith that Christ is your Saviour, then at once you have a gracious God, for faith leads you in and opens up God's heart and will, that you should see pure grace and overflowing love. This is to behold God in faith that you should look upon his fatherly, friendly heart, in which there is no anger nor ungraciousness. He who sees God as angry does not see him rightly but looks only on a curtain, as if a dark cloud had been drawn across his face.[5]

For Luther, this 'tower experience' would mark the beginning of his journey of discovery as a Christian believer. But it did not come all at once. This realization of the meaning of Romans 1:17 would start a chain reaction which would lead to the further development of Reformation doctrine. And Luther would not do it alone. He would have help from other pastors and theologians, who would bring understanding and clarification.

It has been noted that there were three major features to the Protestant understanding of the doctrine of justification. It is to these which we turn next.

Justification is Forensic

The Greek verb *dikaioō* takes center stage, as it is translated in our English Bibles as 'justify.' However, Augustine and some of the church fathers read the Latin translation: *iustificare*, a compound of *iustum* ('just, righteous') and *facere* ('to make'), to arrive at the understanding that the sinner was being *made righteous* in the process of justification.[6] In other words, God is turning the sinner

---

5. Roland H. Bainton, *Here I Stand: A Life of Martin Luther* (Peabody: Hendrickson, 1950), 48.

6. Korey D. Maas, 'Justification by Faith Alone,' in ed. Matthew Barrett, *Reformation Theology: A Systematic Summary* (Wheaton: Crossway, 2017), 516–517. For a fuller discussion of the doctrine of justification as expressed in the early church fathers, see Nathan Busenitz's book, *Long Before Luther:*

into a righteous person in order to save them! But is that Paul's original meaning? Luther didn't believe it was.

For Luther and the Reformers, justification was *forensic* in nature. While this term may sound foreign to us biblically, we certainly understand this term culturally. The word is commonly used in connection to criminal investigations and legal proceedings. That is the same realm of usage here; it refers to the judicial system. R.C. Sproul writes, 'We can reduce its meaning to the concept of *legal declaration*. The doctrine of justification involves a legal matter of the highest order. Indeed, it is the legal issue on which the sinner stands or falls: his status before the supreme tribunal of God.'[7] Humanity is on trial, and God is the judge.

The *forensic* nature of justification is that sinners are *declared righteous* before God. This is a legal act, a verdict handed down by the courts of heaven. Whereas the sinner has nothing in which to boast—no inherent righteousness, nothing to offer, nothing that will please God (cf. Rom. 3:10-18; Isa. 64:6, etc.)—God pardons the sinner, thus treating them as though they are righteous, even though they are *un*righteous.

In truth, God cannot, and will not, declare a person righteous by their own merits because it would be a supreme act of *injustice*! As we've seen, apart from God, humans are terrible law-breakers, unregenerate wretches, sons of disobedience, spiritually dead. No human judge would let a mass murderer go free simply because he paid his taxes on time! In the same way, God will not overlook our trespasses and sins on the basis of our religious activities or our good deeds. He declares, 'by the works of the Law no flesh will be justified in His sight' (Rom. 3:20 NASB). Rather, justification is 'a gift by His grace through the redemption which is in Christ Jesus' (v. 24 NASB). Jesus tells the parable of two men, a Pharisee

---

Tracing the Heart of the Gospel from Christ to the Reformation. (Chicago: Moody Publishers, 2017).

7.   R.C. Sproul, *Faith Alone: The Evangelical Doctrine of Justification* (Grand Rapids: Baker, 1995), 116.

and a tax-collector, who come to worship God in the temple. The Pharisee boasts about his ability to keep God's Law and accomplish a righteousness on his own. But the tax-collector, ashamed of his sin, begs the Lord, 'Be merciful to me, a sinner!' Jesus declares, 'I tell you, this man went down to his house justified rather than the other' (Luke 18:13-14).

While the Lord sits as judge, exercising His decrees, there is a part to be played for those who would be justified. The key element in salvation and justification is *faith*.

According to Hebrews 11:1, faith is 'the assurance of things hoped for, the conviction of things not seen.' Paul makes note of the faith of Abraham, 'being fully assured that what [God] had promised, He was able also to perform' (Rom. 4:21 NASB). It's not what we call 'blind faith,' rather, it is confident belief in the promises of God, and in His ability to keep them. And the Bible says that *faith* is the active agent at work; it is the key that opens the lock. We are justified by faith in Jesus Christ (Rom. 3:28; 5:1; Gal. 3:11, 24), and not by our own efforts to justify ourselves. Even as far back as Genesis 15:6, we see Abraham who 'believed God, and it was credited to him as righteousness.' Luther writes:

> 'Wherefore it ought to be the first concern of every Christian to lay aside confidence in works and increasingly to strengthen faith alone and through faith to grow in the knowledge, not of works, but of Christ Jesus, who suffered and rose for him.'[8]

Sinners are not saved by works, rather, 'by grace [we] have been saved through faith' (Eph. 2:8). And God, who is Himself just, is 'the justifier of the one who has faith in Jesus' (Rom. 3:26).

Justification is Distinct from Sanctification
The second feature of the Protestant understanding of justification is the notion that it is altogether distinct from sanctification.

---

8. Martin Luther, 'The Freedom of a Christian,' in *Three Treatises* (Philadelphia: Fortress, 1970), 281.

According to the *Catechism of the Catholic Church*, 'Justification is conferred in Baptism, the sacrament of faith. It conforms us to the righteousness of God, who makes us inwardly just by the power of his mercy' (§1992). Further, justification is expressed as a cooperative effort: 'Justification establishes *cooperation between God's grace and man's freedom*. On man's part it is expressed by the assent of faith to the Word of God, which invites him to conversion, and in the cooperation of charity with the prompting of the Holy Spirit who precedes and preserves his assent' (§1993). In other words, instead of being a one-time legal declaration, justification is believed to be a process of becoming righteous through a joint effort of God and man. But, is this what the Bible teaches?

In Romans 5:1, Paul speaks of justification in the past tense. He writes, 'Therefore *having been justified by faith*, we have peace with God through our Lord Jesus Christ' (NASB). This points to an already-existing reality in the life of a believer. But it doesn't stop there. Later, in chapter 8, Paul comforts the believer by saying, 'There is therefore now no condemnation for those who are in Christ Jesus' (v. 1). No condemnation—wrath satisfied, fear removed, crisis averted, peace with God. However, he proceeds to instruct the believer to 'walk according to the Spirit' (vv. 4-11), and thereby engage in the process of 'putting to death the deeds of the body' (vv. 12-13 NASB). When we follow Paul's argument, we see that the salvation of the sinner (justification) is a once-for-all-time reality, but the ongoing work of Christian growth (sanctification) is continuous.

At the end of Romans 8, Paul describes this process of becoming 'conformed to the image of [God's] Son' (v. 29). That's what sanctification is: growing in Christlikeness. We see it in Romans 12:2, whereby believers are being 'transformed by the renewing of [their] mind.' Further, we are told that we are 'beholding as in a mirror the glory of the Lord,' and thereby 'being transformed into the same image from glory to glory' (2 Cor. 3:18 NASB). In fact, as Christians, we are to pursue 'sanctification without which no one will see the Lord' (Heb. 12:14 NASB).

But even sanctification is not accomplished through human effort alone. Paul rebukes the Galatians for attempting to become sanctified apart from the work of the Holy Spirit (Gal. 3:1-5). The same Spirit who regenerates the believer unto salvation also takes up residence in them, working to affect their sanctification. John Calvin famously said, 'By partaking of him, we ... receive a double grace: namely, that being reconciled to God through Christ's blamelessness, we may have in heaven instead of a judge a gracious Father; and secondly, that sanctified by Christ's spirit we may cultivate blamelessness and purity of life.'[9]

The problems with confusing or convoluting justification and sanctification are manifold. If justification is not definite, but an ongoing process, there can be no sure basis for salvation, as the believer's future hangs on his ability to perform enough religious works. Frankly, this flies in the face of Christ's work of atonement on the cross. If a believer can gradually justify himself over time, then the cry of Jesus: 'It is finished!' is meaningless (cf. Gal. 2:21). Instead, we are to understand that a person is justified by faith in Jesus Christ, which then produces in them a life of sanctification; good deeds that are pleasing to God (cf. Eph. 2:10; Titus 2:14; 3:8; 1 Pet. 3:13). To summarize: 'With respect to justification, Christ has secured forensic righteousness *for* the believer; in sanctification, the Spirit progressively works practical righteousness *in* the believer.'[10] And though they work together, they are indeed distinct.

Justification is Contingent Upon an Alien Righteousness
The third feature of the Protestant understanding of justification is the notion that believers are justified by God, not based on their own righteousness, but a righteousness that exists outside

---

9. John Calvin, *Institutes of the Christian Religion*, 3.11.1. quoted in Michael Allen, 'Sanctification, Perseverance, and Assurance,' in ed. Matthew Barrett, *Reformation Theology: A Systematic Summary* (Wheaton: Crossway, 2017), 559.

10. John MacArthur and Richard Mayhue, eds. *Biblical Doctrine: A Systematic Summary of Bible Truth* (Wheaton: Crossway, 2017), 632.

themselves—an 'alien' righteousness. One of the key phrases repeated throughout the Reformation was *simul iustus et peccator* ('at the same time just and sinner'). Romans 5 is clear that God justifies persons even 'while [they] are yet sinners' (v. 8); 'while [they] were enemies' (v. 10). Further, even though sinners are justified, they will continue to battle sin for the rest of their earthly life, yet they do not lose their justified status before God (cf. John 10:26-29; Rom. 8:29-39). They are living in the state of having been justified by God, but at the same time, still battling the vestiges of their sin nature.

For Rome, this was a preposterous notion. They could not fathom the idea that a person could be both a sinner and righteous. Instead, they held to the belief that the righteousness of Christ could be *infused* into the believer through partaking in the sacraments, that they could *become* righteous and thereby be justified. However, the Bible explicitly stated that 'none are righteous' (Rom. 3:10), nor could they become righteous by their own efforts (cf. Rom. 10:3). But Luther and the Reformers understood that this was a mysterious biblical reality. And it was all made possible through the *imputation of righteousness*.

Paul explains that God 'made Him who knew no sin to be sin on our behalf, that we might become the righteousness of God in Him' (2 Cor. 5:21 NASB). Jesus Christ, the Righteous One, accomplished a life of perfect, flawless obedience to the Father (Luke 23:47; Heb. 4:15; 7:26; etc.). At the same time, all humanity 'has sinned and fall short of the glory of God' (Rom. 3:23). On the cross, God enacts a phenomenon so provocative, so scandalous, and so foolish (cf. 1 Cor. 1:18ff), it's hard to comprehend. The righteousness of Jesus is credited (or, *imputed*) to the sinner, while the condemnation of the sinner is laid on Christ. Once transacted, Jesus is then punished in the place of the sinner; the sinner is declared righteous based on the merits of Christ. It's been said that, when God looks at Christ on the cross, He sees our sin; but when

He looks at us, He sees the righteousness of Christ. Commenting on *imputation*, Luther writes:

> This is that mystery which is rich in divine grace to sinners, wherein by a wonderful exchange our sins are no longer ours but Christ's, and the righteousness of Christ is not Christ's but ours. He has emptied himself of his righteousness that he might clothe us with it; and fill us with it; and he has taken our evils upon himself that he might deliver us from them.[11]

This 'great exchange' conducted by God serves as the basis for justifying the sinner. In fact, it is the only *legal* way that God is allowed to accept sinners into heaven—through merits of Christ. As we saw earlier, salvation is by 'grace alone' (*sola gratia*) because sinful humanity is utterly incapable of doing good. We have no inherent righteousness that is pleasing to God (Isa. 64:6; Rom. 8:7). We are in need of a righteousness that exists outside ourselves—an 'alien' righteousness; a righteousness that only Jesus Christ can provide.

Luther explains:

> [A Christian] is righteous and holy by an alien or foreign holiness ... that is, he is righteous by the mercy and grace of God. This mercy and grace is not something human; it is not some sort of disposition or quality in the heart. It is a divine blessing, given us through the true knowledge of the Gospel, when we know or believe that our sin has been forgiven through the grace and merit of Christ ... Is not this righteousness an alien righteousness? It consists completely in the indulgence of another and is a pure gift of God, who shows mercy and favor for Christ's sake.[12]

Christians are those who are declared righteous by God, although they are not righteous themselves. 'Sins remain in us, and God

---

11. Johnson, *The Case for Traditional Protestantism*, 91.
12. Sproul, *Faith Alone*, 91.

hates them very much,' said Luther. 'Because of them it is necessary for us to have the imputation of righteousness, which comes to us on account of Christ, who is given to us and grasped by our faith.'[13] It is an astounding reality, and it is all of grace.

John Calvin said:

> 'A man will be justified by faith when, excluded from the righteousness of works, he by faith lays hold of the righteousness of Christ, and clothed in it appears in the sight of God not as a sinner, but as righteous. Thus we simply interpret justification, as the acceptance with which God receives us into his favour as if we were righteous; and we say that this justification consists in the forgiveness of sins and the imputation of the righteousness of Christ.'[14]

How did Rome respond to these bold declarations of biblical truth? Would they come to embrace the Protestant understanding of *justification by faith*?

Rome's Response to *Sola Fide*

In the Augsburg Confession (1530), the first Protestant confession of faith, the Reformers boldly declared their unwavering belief in *sola fide*. In the Confession, Phillip Melanchthon wrote:

> '[M]en cannot be justified before God by their own strength, merits, or works, but are freely justified for Christ's sake, through faith, when they believe that they are received into favour, and that their sins are forgiven for Christ's sake, who, by His death, has made satisfaction for our sins. This faith God imputes for righteousness in His sight.'[15]

---

13. Quoted in Thomas Schreiner, *Faith Alone: The Doctrine of Justification* (Grand Rapids: Zondervan, 2015), 47.

14. John Calvin, *Institutes of the Christian Religion*, trans. Henry Beveridge (1845; Peabody: Hendrickson, 2008), 3.11.2, 475.

15. Article IV, translated by Gerhard Friedrich Bente.

With the opposition growing, Rome made a decisive move. Rather than consider the proposed reforms, they hit back with their own Counter-Reformation. From 1545 to 1563, Catholic leaders met in northern Italy to discuss the points of dispute raised by the Reformers. In the end, they issued a variety of dogmatic decrees and canons, which would include the pronouncement of thirty-three curses on the dissenting views of the doctrine of justification.

During their sixth session, they would pronounce 'anathemas' (curses) on those who would advocate *sola fide*:

> If any one saith, that by faith alone the impious is justified; in such wise as to mean, that nothing else is required to co-operate in order to the obtaining the grace of Justification, and that it is not in any way necessary, that he be prepared and disposed by the movement of his own will; let him be anathema (Canon 9).

> If any one saith, that justifying faith is nothing else but confidence in the divine mercy which remits sins for Christ's sake; or, that this confidence alone is that whereby we are justified; let him be anathema (Canon 12).

These canons and others served to re-double Rome's position, and effectively anathematize those who would maintain *justification by faith apart from works*. What is sadly ironic, however, is the fact that Rome anathematized the very doctrine taught by the apostle Paul in Romans 3 and Galatians 2—what Paul refers to as *his gospel*. And in Galatians 1:8-9, Paul pronounces his own curse on those who would teach a gospel contrary to what he himself taught. By rejecting the doctrine of *justification by faith alone*, Rome placed themselves under the curse of the apostle Paul.

Even today, despite the sweeping changes made in the 1960s with Vatican II, not a single canon of Trent was rescinded; not a word of any decree changed. In fact, four hundred years later, when Pope John XXIII was asked about the decrees, he affirmed: 'What was, still is.'

How Does a Person Get Right With God?

This brings us back to our core question: *How does a person get right with God?* A person must come to realize that they have sinned against a holy God, and that the wages of that sin is death (Rom. 6:23). However, God has made a way, by His grace, to save the sinner, not based on anything righteous that they have done, but by the righteousness possessed and accomplished by Jesus Christ. By faith, the sinner must believe that Jesus went to the cross and died in their place—the innocent for the guilty. By faith (and through repentance), the sinner must believe that the penalty for their life of sin was removed from them and placed on Christ. By faith, the sinner must believe that the perfect righteousness of Christ was credited to their account by God. This 'great exchange' is made by God— a legal declaration, whereby He looks at Christ on the cross and declares, 'Cursed!' and looks at the sinner and declares, 'Justified!' This is what it means to be *justified by faith apart from works*.

Its importance cannot be overstated. It is at the heart of the gospel, which is the only way sinners can be justified before God. Martin Luther affirmed: 'If the article of justification is lost, all Christian doctrine is lost at the same time.'[16]

For we maintain that a person is not justified before God based on their religious observance, or their acts of goodness, or their piety, or their self-denial, or their self-righteousness. The only way we can have a right standing before God is to be justified by His grace alone through faith alone.

In other words, *sola gratia*; *sola fide*.

---

16. Sproul, *Faith Alone*, 84.

I am the way, and the truth, and the life. No one comes to the Father except through Me.
(John 14:6)

5.
Solus Christus
(In Christ Alone)

I n examining our main question: *How does a person get right with God?* we noted that one must be justified (declared righteous) by faith alone in Jesus Christ. That is the essence of *sola gratia* and *sola fide*. However, the Reformers set out to address the issue of the *sufficiency* of the work of Christ. Is there anything else needed? Anything else that must be done? To give a definitive answer, they declared: *solus Christus*—'Christ alone.'

Ulrich Zwingli and the Swiss Reformation

In an amazing providence of God, both German and Swiss Reformations began simultaneously, yet independently, from one another. While Martin Luther has gone down in history as the noted hero of the Protestant movement, the life and ministry of Ulrich Zwingli (1484–1531)[1] is no less significant.

In 1516, when Erasmus' Greek New Testament first appeared in print, Zwingli devoured the text, committing himself to memorizing all of the Pauline Epistles, having copied them down word for word.[2] Zwingli became enamored with the biblical text, captivated by the Word of God. Although he began his ministry as a Roman

---

1.   He is also known as Huldrych Zwingli.

2.   Timothy George, *Theology of the Reformers* (Nashville: B&H, 2013), 116.

Catholic priest, he did not remain a servant of Rome. On January 1, 1519, he was called to the great Minster Church in Zurich, Switzerland. Immediately, he informed his congregation that he would not be delivering the normal 'canned' sermons dictated by the traditional lectionary, but that he would instead preach through the Gospel of Matthew. Zwingli worked aggressively, preaching through Matthew, Acts, 1 and 2 Timothy, Galatians, 1 and 2 Peter, and so on until he had completed the New Testament in 1525. His devotion to the Bible would set a precedent, whereby expository preaching would be established as a fundamental practice in the Reformation.

A deepening commitment to expository preaching quickly revealed a plethora of problems with the theology and practice of Roman Catholicism. While growing in boldness and zeal, Zwingli launched his first attack on the practices of the Church in 1522, specifically on the custom of fasting during Lent. Soon after, he attacked the displaying of religious images in church buildings. In August 1523, he penned, *An Attack on the Canon of the Mass*, calling for its removal. The attack on the Mass plunged Zwingli and all of Zurich into an uproar, and he soon debated the bishop of Constance, ultimately winning over the local magistrates. Subsequently, on April 12, 1525, the Mass was effectively abolished in Zurich.

The basis for Zwingli's robust opposition to Roman Catholic dogma was rooted in his exalted view of Scripture, and his fervent love for Jesus Christ. He saw the pervasive veneration of images and relics as nothing short of idolatry—a full-on assault on the glory of Christ. Timothy George notes, 'No one preached *solus Christus* more strongly than he,'[3] as Zwingli himself proclaimed, 'Christ is the only way to salvation for all who ever were, are and shall be.'[4] And he believed Roman Catholicism to be the epitome of anti-gospel.

---

3. ibid., 129.

4. Quoted in George, *Theology of the Reformers*, 124.

In response to Zwingli's teaching, the churches in Zurich were emptied of all their religious relics, images, and Catholic paraphernalia. Windows were smashed, pipe organs were removed, altars were torn down. In a letter to Emperor Charles V, Johann Eck described the state of the Swiss churches: 'The altars are destroyed and overthrown, the images of the saints and the paintings are burned or broken up or defaced ... They no longer have churches but rather stables.'[5] But Zwingli cared nothing for the former glory of the church buildings; he cared only for the glory of Christ. Commenting on his war on idolatry, he confessed, 'I call my flock absolutely away, as far as I can, from hope in any created being to the one true God and Jesus his only begotten Son.'[6]

By this time, all of Europe knew the name of Martin Luther. And Zwingli greatly admired Luther and the other Reformers, even referring to him as an 'Elijah' in his debates against Johann Eck in Leipzig.[7] Despite his admiration of the German Reformer, Zwingli insisted, 'I did not learn my doctrine from Luther, but from God's Word itself.'[8] At first, Luther and Zwingli were allies, even corresponding back and forth. But soon, disagreement arose between them. While they agreed on many important points of doctrine, their largest contention was over the meaning of the Lord's Supper. Both men wrote fierce attacks on one another, debating the issue on the public square.

Finally, in an effort to bring about a truce, Prince Philip of Hesse attempted to negotiate a peace between the two men. In 1529, both men along with their associates, met in Marburg, Germany. After three days of discussion and debate, they emerged united on fourteen major points of doctrine. However, the last issue to be discussed—the Lord's Supper—left them divided. Luther, although denying the Roman Catholic doctrine of *transubstantiation*,

5. ibid., 135.

6. ibid., 125.

7. George, *Theology of the Reformers*, 117.

8. ibid.

developed the view of *consubstantiation*, the belief that Christ was spiritually present *with* the sacramental elements of the bread and wine. Zwingli, on the other hand, maintained that Jesus' words, 'This is my body' (Matt. 26:26; etc.) were meant to be taken figuratively. His view was that the Lord's Supper was a *memorial* observance, merely *signifying* the body and blood of Christ. Both were unable to convince the other of their position. On the last day, as Luther got up to exit the meeting, Zwingli cried out in tears, 'There are no people on earth with whom I would rather be in harmony than with the Wittenbergers.'[9] Sadly, the two would never reconcile. Zwingli would die on the battlefield two years later, in 1531, as a chaplain for the Swiss army.

Despite the quarrel between Luther and Zwingli, as well as some of Zwingli's radical views and practices, we have an example of an earnest believer, transfixed on the glory of Christ. Further, his belief in *solus Christus* (salvation in 'Christ alone') no doubt blossomed out of his belief in *sola Scriptura*. He maintained:

> We know from the Old and New Testaments of God that our only comforter, redeemer, savior, and mediator with God is Jesus Christ, in whom and through alone we can obtain grace, help and salvation, and besides from no other being in heaven or on earth.[10]

And so, in following his example, we seek to behold the glory of Christ displayed in the Word of God.

Jesus Christ: Our Lord and Savior

Jesus proclaimed that the Scriptures 'bear witness of Me' (John 5:39 NASB). For us, we understand the person and work of Jesus Christ through our understanding of the Word of God (cf. Luke 24:27). While inexhaustible volumes could be written about Christ

---

9.   S.M. Houghton, *Sketches in Church History: An Illustrated Account of 20 Centuries of Christ's Power* (Edinburgh: Banner of Truth Trust, 1980), 100.

10. Quoted in George, *Theology of the Reformers*, 134.

(John 21:25), for our purposes, we'll take a brief look at *who He is* and *what He has done.*

His Person: Who He is

In John's prologue (John 1:1-18), we are immediately faced with the magnificent reality that Jesus Christ (called, 'The Word' in verses 1 and 14) is *pre-existent* and *co-equal* with God the Father; He is the *co-creator* of the universe (cf. Col. 1:15-18), and the *source* of all light and life. In short, He is God Himself; the Second Person of the Trinity. But then, we read that He 'became flesh and dwelt among us' (v. 14). The infinite became finite; deity took on humanity (Phil. 2:7). Yet, we understand that He possesses two natures in one—*deity* and *humanity.*

We read in Matthew's and Luke's Gospel that Jesus was born of the Virgin Mary. And while, according to Romans 5:12, sin and death are passed down to all of humanity through Adam, in the case of Jesus, being 'born of the Holy Spirit' (Matt. 1:18), He was not conceived in sin. Jesus was not born with a sin nature, nor did He commit sins during His lifetime (2 Cor. 5:21; 1 Pet. 2:22; 1 John 3:5). But apart from being born sinless, Jesus is human in every way. The Gospels point to His humanity: He worked, He sweat, He ate, He slept, He laughed, He cried, He bled, He died, etc. Jesus is human.

But He is also God.

Over and over again, Scripture teaches us of the deity of Christ. Jesus is superior to angels (Heb. 1:5-14), transcendent above all creation; He is the uncreated One. In John 8:58, Jesus proclaims, 'Before Abraham was born, I AM'—invoking the very name of God given in the Old Testament. In John 10:30, Jesus claims equality with God; 'I and the Father are one.' He startles the religious leaders in Mark 2, when He declares that He can forgive sins—an act reserved only for God (v. 7). He spoke with the authority of God (Matt. 7:29). He demonstrated the power of God (Mark 4:36-41; etc.). He was worshiped as God (Matt. 2:2, 11;

14:33; John 9:35-38). And when Thomas sees Jesus again after the Resurrection, he declares, 'My Lord and My God'(John 20:28). Titus 2:13 calls Jesus, 'our great *God* and Savior.'

Jesus is the God-man: God in human flesh. And He came to earth on a mission.

His Work: What He has done

While on earth, Jesus of Nazareth lived as a man, indistinguishable from every other man alive, except that He never once transgressed the law of God. He obeyed every rule, fulfilled every command, completed every task— perfectly. He never sinned by way of commission, or by omission. He never said a hateful word, He never thought an evil thought. He only ever committed righteous deeds. In fact, He is the *only* one in the history of humanity to do it. He accomplished a perfectly righteous life, and the Father was pleased (Matt. 3:17; 17:5; John 8:29). This is what scholars call His *active obedience*. Were Jesus to ascend back to heaven at the end of His life, He would have been welcomed based on His own merits. But we know that Jesus came to do more; He came to give His life for many.

The Jewish leadership, in league with the Romans, arrested Jesus, tried Him for blasphemy, whipped Him severely, and sent Him to His death—death on a Roman cross. However, Jesus declared, 'No one takes my life from Me, but I lay it down on My own initiative. I have the authority to lay it down, and I have authority to take it up again' (John 10:18). And so, Jesus willingly offered Himself up to die. But, why? Because through His death, He would accomplish a work that no one else could accomplish.

First, Jesus accomplished the work of *substitution*. He died *in the place of* sinners. Isaiah, speaking of Jesus, prophesied that the Messiah would be 'pierced *for* our transgressions' and 'crushed *for* our iniquities' (53:5, emphasis mine). Peter writes, 'He Himself bore our sins in His body on the tree, that we might die to sin and live to righteousness' (1 Pet. 2:24). As Paul says of Christ's taking on our punishment: '[He] who knew no sin [became] sin on our behalf, that we might become the righteousness of God in Him' (2 Cor. 5:21 NASB). In short, Jesus died *in our place*, as a substitute.

Second, Jesus accomplished the work of *redemption*. Through Christ's death on the cross, He paid a ransom to the Father for us (Mark 10:45). He redeemed us. In 1 Corinthians 6:20, we learn that we 'have been bought with a price.' We owed a sin-debt to God that we could not pay; the only outcome is eternal punishment in hell. But Jesus paid our fine—'redeemed us from the curse of the Law' (Gal. 3:13), thus securing our freedom (John 8:36; Rom. 8:2). Therefore, He has ransomed us; He has redeemed us.

Third, Jesus accomplished the work of *propitiation*. While this word is not commonly used much in everyday vernacular, we know from Scripture that it has to do with satisfying God's righteousness, including God's anger against the sinner (1 John 2:2; 4:10). Christ's atoning sacrifice was pleasing to God, as God was able to justify the sinner 'through the redemption which is in Christ Jesus' (Rom. 3:24). Whereas the blood of bulls and goats were unable to satisfy God's wrath against sin (Heb. 9:12; 10:1-4), the sacrifice of Jesus Christ was sufficient.

Fourth, Jesus accomplished the *forgiveness* of sins. All the sacrifices, all the prayers, all the fasting, all the self-deprecation, and all the good deeds in the world cannot accomplish the forgiveness of sins. Only the death of Christ can remove the guilt of sin (*expiation*), and reconcile us to God. Because of Christ, God has 'forgiven us all our transgressions' (Col. 2:13).

Fifth, Jesus brought about our *justification*. On the cross, Christ took away the penalty of our sin debt (Col. 2:14), and was judged. At the same time, His righteousness was *imputed* to the sinner as a gift by faith (2 Cor. 5:21). Because of Christ—and *Christ alone*—God can pardon the sinner, thus declaring them *justified*.

Additionally, His resurrection from the grave on the third day has provided: the proof that God has accepted His sacrifice (Rom. 3:25; cf. Isa. 53:10), hope for our own regeneration

(1 Pet. 1:3), hope for our own justification (Rom. 4:25), a model of our future bodily resurrection (1 Cor. 6:14), and power to be granted to the believer to live righteously (Rom. 6:10-11; 8:11-13). In short, the resurrection of Jesus Christ brings new life to all who believe—in this present life and in the life to come.

The testimony of Scripture is undeniable. No other means or method, no other agent or savior, can provide the redemption, salvation, regeneration, justification, and resurrection needed for the believer. Only Christ, and *Christ alone*.

However, the Reformers recognized that the Roman Catholic system presented many affronts to the work of Christ— opposition that needed to be countered in order to preserve the true, biblical gospel.

Affronts to *Solus Christus*

Roman Catholicism is a complex system, full of nuance. And while both Protestants and Catholics affirm salvation through Jesus Christ, Catholicism does not affirm that it comes through Christ *alone*. Rather, they teach that there exists a number of other persons and processes to aid in the salvation of the believer.

The Mass

According to the *Catechism of the Catholic Church*, 'The sacrifice of Christ and the sacrifice of the Eucharist are one single sacrifice: In this divine sacrifice which is celebrated in the Mass, the same Christ who offered himself once in a bloody manner on the altar of the cross is contained and is offered in an unbloody manner' (§1367). During the worship service—the Mass—the bread and wine (Eucharist) are believed to be transformed into the 'living and glorious' body and blood of Jesus Christ. What is known as the doctrine of *transubstantiation*, teaches that Christ 'is present in a true, real, and substantial manner: his Body and his Blood, with his soul and his divinity' (§1413). Upon the priest's command, the bread and wine are transformed into Christ, wherein He is re-offered up as a sacrifice for sin.

However, Hebrews 9:26 tells us that Christ has already appeared 'to put away sin by the sacrifice of Himself,' and 'having offered one sacrifice for sins for all time, sat down at the right hand of God' (10:12 NASB). The Bible teaches that the once-for-all-sacrifice of Christ is enough to atone for all sins—past, present, and future. Further, Jesus' final words on the cross were, 'It is finished' (John 19:30)—a definitive cry of accomplishment. The sacrificial system laid out in Leviticus was stopped, no other sacrifices would be needed.

What about when Jesus declared that believers were to 'eat [His] flesh and drink [His] blood' in John 6? The obvious answer is that Jesus was speaking metaphorically, since the Jews were prohibited from drinking blood, certainly human blood! Rather, Jesus was speaking of the intimacy of fellowship believers needed to have with Him; the close intimacy of eating and drinking. Elsewhere, Jesus used other metaphors, proclaiming, 'I am the light of the world' (John 8:12), 'I am the door' (John 10:7, 9), 'I am the good shepherd' (John 10:11, 14), 'I am the resurrection and the life'(John 11:25); He also claimed, 'I am the bread of life' (John 6:35) and believers were to partake in close fellowship with Him.

But even if the bread and wine were magically turned into the literal body and blood of Jesus Christ to be offered up in 'an unbloody manner,' the sacrifice itself would still be insufficient, as Hebrews 9:22 says, 'all things are cleansed with blood, and without the shedding of blood there is no forgiveness of sins.' Even if transubstantiation were possible, not a single sin could be cleansed. For not even 'the blood of bulls and goats' is sufficient (Heb. 10:4); only the unique and all-sufficient sacrifice of the perfect Savior on the cross of Calvary can provide true atonement.

The Saints and the 'Treasury of Merit'

One of the most common practices of Catholics is to entreat the help of saints who have passed on, in hopes of obtaining grace through the benefits of their extra works. However, if we understand that 'none are righteous' (Rom. 3:10; cf. Isa. 64:6), and the only righteousness available to the believer is the *imputed righteousness* of Christ, then all the 'merit' possessed by the saints of church history is not their own; it all belongs to Christ, because the good deeds done are done *in Christ* (Eph. 2:10; cf. 1 Cor. 6:19-20). And so, to access a 'treasury of merit' is simply to access an endless well of Christ's righteousness; and no other person can add their own righteousness to it. Therefore, praying to saints is wrong, asking for their intercession is futile, and attempting to draw from the treasury of their good deeds is impossible.

Mary: Another Savior?

Next to the Lord Jesus Christ, it is believed that the Virgin Mary possesses authority to ensure believers will enter heaven. Roman Catholic dogma teaches that Mary was born 'preserved immune from all stain of original sin' (§491), that she was miraculously assumed into heaven without dying (§966), and currently intercedes for the Church, bringing 'the gifts of eternal salvation' to believers, and functions as our 'Advocate, Helper, Benefactress, and Mediatrix' (§969).

But Scripture teaches nothing of the sort. While Mary was blessed with the joy of carrying the Lord Jesus Christ, she is no different than any other believer. In Luke 1:46–55, we see Mary's total submission to the Lord, as she prepares to give birth to Jesus. However, she is seldom mentioned throughout the New Testament, last appearing in Acts 1:14, before disappearing from the pages of Scripture. Nowhere in Acts or the Epistles is it taught that she was sinless, or assumed into heaven, or has any part in the work of salvation whatsoever. She is not mentioned in Paul's or John's epistles, nor did the early church teach that Mary had any part to play in salvation or intercession. To believe that Mary is some kind of *co-redeemer* is false at best, blasphemous at worst.

The Pope

The Roman Catholic Church teaches that its priests serve as mediators to absolve sin through administering the sacraments. And sitting at the top of the whole order is the Pope. As we saw earlier, it is believed that when the Pope speaks *ex cathedra* he is speaking for God, and therefore, he is infallible. But beyond merely claiming to speak for God, it is believed he is also acting as Christ's representative. According to their *Catechism*, 'the Roman Pontiff, by reason of his office as Vicar of Christ, and as pastor of the entire Church has full, supreme, and universal power over the whole Church, a power which he can always exercise unhindered' (§882). Let's examine a few of these claims.

The Pope is said to be the *Vicar of Christ* on earth, that is, he is Christ's substitute or representative. The belief is that, when Jesus ascended to heaven, He left Peter as the first Pope (followed by the papal succession) to serve in His place as leader of the Church. But this dogma is rife with problems. Martin Luther explains,

> See how different Christ is from his successors, although they all would wish to be his vicars. I fear that most of them have been too literally his vicars. A man is a vicar only when his superior is absent. If the Pope rules, while Christ is absent and does not dwell in his heart, what else is he but a vicar of Christ? What is the church under such a vicar but a mass of people without Christ? Indeed, what is such a vicar but an antichrist and an idol? How much more properly did the apostles call themselves servants of the present Christ and not vicars of an absent Christ.[11]

In other words, the presence of a human *vicar*, or substitute, would only be probable if Christ were not still present within His church. But in John 14, Jesus specifically tells the disciples, 'I will ask the Father, and He will give you another Helper [*paraklētos*: comforter,

---

11. Martin Luther, 'The Freedom of a Christian,' in *Three Treatises* (Philadelphia: Fortress, 1970), 275.

counselor, exhorter, intercessor, encourager, and advocate[12]], that He may be with you forever— that is, the Spirit of truth' (vv. 16-17a; cf. John 16:7-15). In the place of the Son, the Father would send the Holy Spirit. Jesus continues, 'You know Him because He abides with you, and *will be in you*' (v. 17b NASB, emphasis added). Who is the *Vicar of Christ*, the substitute who leads the church in His place? It is none other than the Holy Spirit who indwells the members of Christ's church.

The Pope is also said to be *The Supreme Pontiff*. Derived from the Latin word *pontifex*, the term refers to a 'bridge,' or a 'bridge-builder.' Historically, the term was used of the Roman Caesar— the *pontifex maximus*—to describe the one who presides over the government of the Holy Roman Empire. Within a few centuries, this position of power was transferred to the Bishop of Rome, thus investing him with the supreme powers of leading the Church and the State. But, is the Roman Pontiff the true head of the church, and the 'bridge' between heaven and earth?

First Timothy 2:5 tells us that there is 'one mediator between God and men, the man Christ Jesus' (cf. Heb. 7:25). First John 2:1-2 says, 'we have an Advocate with the Father,' and it is not an earthly leader, it is 'Jesus Christ the righteous.' In John 1:51, Jesus claims to be the ladder in Jacob's vision, the connector ['bridge'] between heaven and earth. He's the Mediator, the Advocate, the Bridge. Further, Colossians 1:18 tells us that Christ is also 'the head of the body, the church.' And so, Jesus Christ is the *Supreme Pontiff*, if there ever was one.

Lastly, the supreme leader of the Roman Catholic Church is called *The Pope*. The word 'Pope' comes from the Latin word *papa*, which means 'father.' And when he is addressed, the Pope is called 'The Holy Father.' However, in His vicious diatribe against the Pharisees, Jesus instructed His disciples, 'Do not call anyone on earth your father; for only One is your Father, He who is in heaven'

---

12. John MacArthur, *John 12-21*. The MacArthur New Testament Commentary. (Chicago: Moody, 2008), 112.

(Matt. 23:9 NASB). Further, speaking of Himself, He continued, 'And do not be called leaders; for only One is your Leader, that is, Christ' (v. 10). Jesus rebukes anyone who would refer to religious leaders as 'father' or even 'leader,' rather, He says, 'But the greatest among you shall be your servant' (v. 11). According to Jesus, the greatest church leaders are those who humble themselves before others and claim nothing but the title of 'servant' (cf. Matt. 20:26; Phil. 2:3-4).

Based on the testimony of Scripture, it is clear that the various titles for, and even the existence of the Pope, explicitly blaspheme the Persons of the Trinity: the Father, the Son, and the Holy Spirit.[13] According to Ulrich Zwingli, 'Christ is the only eternal high priest, wherefrom it follows that those who have called themselves high priests have opposed the honor and power of Christ, yea, cast it out.'[14] Luther went even further:

> 'The Pope is not the head of all Christendom by divine right or according to God's word ... [Rather] the Pope is the real Antichrist who has raised himself over and set himself against Christ, for the Pope will not permit people to be saved except by his own power, which amounts to nothing since it is neither established nor commanded by God. This is actually what St. Paul calls exalting oneself over and against God.'[15]

But we are not saved through the work of an anti-Christ. We are saved only by the sufficient work of the true Christ.

---

13. This concept of the Trinitarian blasphemy was derived from an interview with Phillip Jensen at the 2016 Together for the Gospel Conference. www.phillipjensen.com/video/mark-dever-interviews-phillip-jensen-at-together-for-the-gospel-2016/.

14. Ulrich Zwingli, 'The Sixty-Seven Articles (1523),' in Stephen Wellum, *Christ Alone: The Uniqueness of Jesus as Savior* (Grand Rapids: Zondervan, 2017), 268.

15. Quoted in Kim Riddlebarger, 'Eschatology,' in ed. Matthew Barrett, *Reformation Theology: A Systematic Summary* (Wheaton: Crossway, 2017), 736.

Affirming *Solus Christus*

The distinguishing mark of Martin Luther's theology was what he called 'the theology of the cross.' In short, it was a biblical worldview built on the notion that all of life, all of theology, all of existence, all of our knowledge of God, and all of salvation must be viewed through Christ's work on the cross. Similarly, the apostle Paul declared, 'For I determined to know nothing among you except Jesus Christ, and Him crucified' (1 Cor. 2:2 NASB).

It is all about Christ, and *Christ alone.*

He is our Prophet, He is our Priest, and He is our King.

'And there is salvation in no one else; for there is no other name under heaven been given among men, by which we must be saved' (Acts 4:12).

The door to heaven is only as wide as the shoulders of Jesus Christ; for He declared, 'I am the way, and the truth, and the life; no one comes to the Father, except through Me' (John 14:6).

We affirm that Christ 'is the radiance of [God's] glory and the exact representation of His nature, and upholds all things by the word of His power. [And] when *He* had made purification of sins, He sat down at the right hand of the Majesty on high' (Heb. 1:3 NASB, emphasis added).

We do not look to earthly saviors, nor do we rely on the intercession of saints. Neither *religious rituals* nor *pious prayers* nor *earthly sacrifices* nor *extravagant offerings* nor *human merits* can accomplish the work of salvation.

Only Christ, and *Christ alone.*

And at the name of Jesus, every knee should bow and every tongue should confess that Jesus Christ is the all-sufficient Lord and Savior, to the glory of God the Father. Amen.

For from Him and through Him and to Him are all things.
To Him be the glory forever. Amen.
(Romans 11:36)

6.
Soli Deo Gloria
(For the Glory of God Alone)

All along we have been asking: *How does a person get right with God?* We have affirmed that, according to *Scripture alone*, salvation is *by God's grace alone* through *faith alone* in *Christ alone*. But this God-centered view of salvation is not meant to produce lazy Christians who sit around and merely bask in the notion that they've been justified by faith apart from any works. It is not meant to produce a dead faith which lacks obedience (cf. James 2:14-26). Rather, all of the Christian life exists for the expressed purpose of bringing glory to God. Yes, all things are to be done for the glory of God alone—*soli Deo gloria*.

John Calvin and *Coram Deo*
Aside from Martin Luther, there is no Reformer who has had a larger impact on Christianity than John Calvin. In the early years of the French Reformation, Cardinal Sadolet penned a letter to the leaders in Geneva, Switzerland, pleading with them to return to the Roman Catholic Church. It would be the written response of the young Calvin that would echo throughout all of Europe. John Piper notes, 'The issue [was] not, first, the well-known sticking points of the Reformation: justification, priestly abuses, transubstantiation, prayers to saints, and papal authority ... But beneath all of them, the

fundamental issue for John Calvin ... was the issue of *the centrality and supremacy and majesty of the glory of God*.'[1] This would remain his concern throughout his entire life.

John Calvin was born in July, 1509 in Picardy, France. Unlike Martin Luther, who defied his father to pursue theology instead of law, Calvin obeyed his father, and gave up studying theology to become a lawyer.[2] Early on, Calvin set himself apart as a model student, driven and meticulous. And God would use his gifts in a mighty way.

While many can trace their conversion to a distinct moment, Calvin's salvation seems to be a more gradual awakening to the things of God. By Calvin's own testimony, Bruce Gordon notes that 'he had been brought up a Christian, and that his conversion was essentially a shift of allegiance from the Church of Rome to the Word of God.'[3] However, he describes his own conversion as 'sudden,' noting, 'I was immediately inflamed with so intense a desire to make progress therein, that although I did not altogether leave off other studies, yet I pursued them with less ardour.'[4] In his realization of the glory of God, he would later articulate his belief that all of life is lived *Coram Deo*—always and ever 'before God.'

Soon after becoming a Christian, Calvin aligned himself with the Reformation effort in France. On November 1, 1533, Nicholas Cop, a friend of Calvin and rector of the University of Paris, gave a controversial sermon against the Roman Catholic Church that sent the city into an uproar. Cop, along with Calvin who was in the audience, would flee Paris and make their way to the city of Basel. It was there that Calvin began to minister, and publish the first edition of his *Institutes of the Christian Religion* in 1536. The

1.   John Piper, *John Calvin and His Passion for the Majesty of God* (Wheaton: Crossway, 2009), 15-16.

2.   Timothy George, *Theology of the Reformers*. (Nashville: B&H, 2013), 178.

3.   Bruce Gordon, *Calvin* (New Haven: Yale University Press, 2009), 33.

4.   Cited in Steven J. Lawson, *The Expository Genius of John Calvin*. A Long Line of Godly Men Profile. (Orlando: Reformation Trust, 2007), 8.

work would see four more revisions during his lifetime, but Calvin's initial purpose for it was to act as a theological primer for French citizens, those, he writes, 'whom I saw to be hungering and thirsting for Christ.'[5]

In the summer of 1536, on a trip to Strasbourg, Calvin was unexpectedly detoured to the city of Geneva, where longtime Reformer Guillaume Farel would plead with him to stay on as a church leader in the city. At first, Calvin declined, but Farel proved too persuasive, and Calvin relented, staying on to help with the work. He writes:

> Farel, who burned with an extraordinary zeal to advance the gospel, immediately strained every nerve to detain me. And after he had learned that my heart was set upon devoting myself to private studies, and finding that entreaties were in vain, he went on to say that God would curse my retirement and the peace of study that I sought, if I withdrew and refused him my help when the need of it was so urgent. I was so terror-stricken that I abandoned the journey I had planned; but I was so sensible of my natural shyness and timidity that I would not bind myself to accept any particular office.[6]

However, the torch would later be passed from Farel to Calvin, who would soon lead the Reformation, not only in Geneva, but throughout the whole known world.

The work in Geneva was challenging and laborious. In light of the people's commitment to live 'according to the law of the gospel and the Word of God,'[7] Calvin was adamant that the people not simply be Christians by profession, but also by action. After all, they were living *Coram Deo*—'before God,' sitting in the midst of

---

5.   Quoted in George, *Theology of the Reformers*, 185.

6.   S.M. Houghton, *Sketches in Church History*. (Edinburgh: Banner of Truth Trust, 1980), 104-105.

7.   George, *Theology of the Reformers*, 186.

God's 'theater of divine glory.'[8] But many Genevans, namely the Libertines, resented Calvin's calls for holiness, and both he and Farel were ousted from the city in 1538.

From Geneva, Calvin was invited by Martin Bucer to Strasbourg, where he would spend three joyous years. While in Strasbourg, he would pastor a church, revise his *Institutes*, begin writing Bible commentaries, and take a wife, a lovely woman named Idelette. Life seemed perfect in Strasbourg, but soon, Geneva came crawling back to him.

Having regretted their decision to remove him, the magistrates of Geneva pursued Calvin and pled with him to return as their pastor. As before, he was reluctant to do so, but eventually agreed to come back. On September 13, 1541, John Calvin returned to Geneva, where he would stay for the rest of his life. On the first Sunday since his removal, the people expected a tirade from him, but Calvin simply walked up to the pulpit, and began to preach from the text he left off with three years earlier.

Life in Geneva had its challenges. Idelette gave birth to Calvin's only son, who died at two weeks old. After losing his child, Calvin wrote to his friend, Pierre Viret, 'The Lord has certainly inflicted a severe and bitter wound in the death of our baby son. But He is Himself a Father and knows best what is good for his children.'[9] Even in death, Calvin submitted himself to the Lord. A few short years later, Idelette died of tuberculosis, leaving Calvin a widower. However, Idelette had two other children from her first husband, for whom he would continue to care, as well as some of his own nieces and nephews from his brother Antoine. In the midst of all the challenges, Calvin devoted himself to his studies, to his church, and to his Lord.

---

8. John Calvin, *Institutes of the Christian Religion*, 1.15.3. in David Vandrunen, *God's Glory Alone: The Majestic Heart of Christian Faith and Life* (Grand Rapids: Zondervan, 2015), 19.

9   Parker, *Portrait of Calvin*, 71 in John Piper, *John Calvin and His Passion for the Majesty of God* (Wheaton: Crossway, 2009), 36.

Geneva soon became ground zero for the Protestant Reformation. Upon his return, Calvin drew up a *Church Order*, a set of rules for church governance. This would serve to govern all religious life in the city. In addition to ministering to his own people, however, Calvin ministered to refugees who fled to the city from other parts of Europe. Geneva became the temporary home of John Knox from Scotland, as well as about two-hundred refugees from England. Both the English and Scottish Reformation efforts were directly impacted by the ministry in Geneva.

The year 1559 saw the founding of the Geneva Academy, as well as the final edition of Calvin's *Institutes*, hailed as 'the greatest exposition of evangelical truth produced by the Reformation.'[10] Additionally, a new Bible translation was published in 1560, the Geneva Bible, which would serve as the favorite translation for the Reformers and the Puritans over the next 100 years. Calvin published commentaries on nearly every book of the New Testament, and several on books in the Old Testament. He preached more than 2,000 sermons in Geneva, many of which are still in print today.

By 1558, Calvin's health began to decline, leaving his disciple, Theodore Beza, to shoulder much of the work in Geneva. After battling many health issues, John Calvin died on May 27, 1564 at the age of fifty-four. In his final words, he maintained:

> Concerning my doctrine, I have taught faithfully and God has given me the grace to write. I have done this as faithfully as possible and have not corrupted a single passage of Scripture, nor knowingly twisted it ... I have never written anything from hatred of anyone, but have always faithfully set before me what I deemed to be the glory of God.[11]

---

10. B.K. Kuiper, *The Church in History* (Grand Rapids: Eerdmans, 1951), 191.

11. Quoted in George, *Theology of the Reformers*, 256.

While being far from a perfect man, John Calvin gave his all to live faithfully before God—*Coram Deo*, and labored to do all things to the glory of God alone.

But, where did he arrive at his belief that all of life should exist for the glory of God? From none other than the pages of Scripture.

The Glory of God in Scripture

When Jesus sat down and talked with the woman at the well, He explained to her, 'God is spirit' (John 4:24), implying that He could not be visited at a temple or observed like a statue. He is vast, omnipresent, majestic, radiant; like the wind, He moves mysteriously (cf. John 3:8). However, Scripture bears witness to the fact that God can be realized; He can be seen, though heavily veiled. From Genesis to Revelation, the Lord God is comprehended most through the beholding of His glory.

The Radiance of God's Glory

The Hebrew word translated 'glory' or 'glorious' is *kabowd*, and it means honor or splendor— 'something worthy of praise or exaltation; brilliance; beauty; renown.'[12] The glory of God is the manifestation of His person and presence.

Throughout the Old Testament, we see visible images of God's glory. In Exodus 3, Moses encounters the Lord in the burning bush; an image of God as an all-consuming fire (cf. Exod. 24:17; Heb. 12:29). As the Israelites were led out of Egypt, we read that 'the Lord was going before them in a pillar of cloud by day to lead them on the way, and in a pillar of fire by night to give them light' (Exod. 13:21 NASB). For them, God was ever-present; a cloud of protection and fire of light. However, when the people complained against the Lord in Exodus 16, they watched as 'the glory of the Lord appeared in the cloud' (v. 10 NASB).

---

12. John MacArthur, *Worship: The Ultimate Priority* (Chicago: Moody, 2012), 166.

But even during these difficult years, God desired to dwell with His people. After the construction of the tabernacle, we read, 'Then the cloud covered the tent of meeting, and the glory of the Lord filled the tabernacle' (Exod. 40:34). Despite the fact that God is spirit, He made His glory to dwell within the realm of earthly space. And God's glory would remain in the tabernacle, and later in the temple, to demonstrate to His people that He was with them. And the saddest day in their early history was when the Ark of the Covenant was stolen, and the glory of God departed from Israel (1 Sam. 4:21-22).

A Display of God's Glory

Moses encounters the glory of the Lord on Mount Sinai. After pleading with God to forgive the sins of His people, Moses asks God, 'I pray You, show me Your glory!' Up to that point, he had spoken with God openly, but desired a closer connection, more intimacy. We read:

> But [the Lord] said, 'You cannot see My face, for no man can see Me and live!' Then the Lord said, 'Behold, there is a place by Me, and you shall stand there on the rock; and it will come about, while My glory is passing by, that I will put you in the cleft of the rock and cover you with My hand until I have passed by. Then I will take My hand away and you shall see My back, but My face shall not be seen' (Exod. 33:20-23 NASB).

And so, in the very next chapter, we read that the Lord came down in the cloud, and Moses cried out to God.

> Then the Lord passed by in front of him and proclaimed, 'The Lord, the Lord God, compassionate and gracious, slow to anger, and abounding in lovingkindness and truth; who keeps lovingkindness for thousands, who forgives iniquity, transgression and sin; yet He will by no means leave the guilty unpunished, visiting the iniquity

of fathers on the children and on the grandchildren to the third and fourth generations' (Exod. 34:6-7 NASB).

What is Moses' response to seeing and hearing God? He quickly bowed down and worshiped (v. 8).

What is fascinating about this encounter is the two-fold display of God's glory. First, we see the *visible* display of glory—the Lord passes by in a radiant flash of light! In fact, the glory of God is so bright, Moses' face absorbs its brightness and he must cover his face with a veil so that the people can look at him.

However, there is a second component to Moses' encounter with God. As He passes by him, the Lord proclaims His own *name* and declares His *attributes*. He emphasizes, 'The Lord, the Lord God"—His proper name, 'Yahweh! Yahweh!' And then He begins to list various aspects of His character and nature. Specifically, He makes note of His compassion, graciousness, forbearance, lovingkindness, truthfulness, forgiveness, and justice. More than simply showing Moses a visible display, brighter than ten thousand suns, He offers him a summary of all that He is—the sum of His divine attributes.

Further, the Lord displays His glory through what He has made—the creation. 'The heavens are telling of the glory of God; and their expanse is declaring the work of His hands' (Ps. 19:1 NASB). The beauty and majesty of creation, much like the radiant glow on Moses' face, give just a hint of the awesome splendor of the Lord. John Calvin writes:

> 'There is no part of the world, however small, in which at least some spark of God's glory does not shine. In particular, we cannot gaze upon this beautiful masterpiece of the world, in all its length and breadth, without being completely dazzled, as it were, by an endless flood of light.'[13]

---

13. John Calvin, *Institutes of the Christian Religion*, trans. Robert White (1541; reprint, Edinburgh: Banner of Truth Trust, 2014), 10.

Giving Glory to God

So far, we have only seen God's *intrinsic* glory—the glory that belongs to Him—that of His person and presence. However, there exists in Scripture the mandate to 'give glory to God.' But, how do you give God anything? Surely, you could not add glory to His nature!

Psalm 29 commands us to 'Ascribe to the Lord glory and strength ... the glory due to His name' (cf. 1 Chr. 16:28, 29). This word translated 'ascribe' means to give, provide, or render. However, the sense is not that we give to God what He already possesses; rather, that we recognize and acknowledge His glory. God is jealous for His glory (and rightfully so); He proclaims, 'I will not give My glory to another!' (Isa. 42:8 NASB). God desires that His creation acknowledge its Creator and worship Him for who He is and for what He has done.

God's Glory in Christ Jesus

The ultimate display of God's glory came through the sending of His Son, the Lord Jesus Christ. For we know that 'He is the image of the invisible God' (Col. 1:15), 'the radiance of [God's] glory and the exact representation of His nature' (Heb. 1:3 NASB). It was as though the magnificent glory cloud that passed by Moses was squeezed into the body of Jesus of Nazareth, in whom dwells the fullness of God (Col. 1:19; cf. John 1:1-3, 16). He was born in glory (Luke 2:9, 14), He died in glory (John 13:31), and He rose to life in glory (Rom. 6:4).

John declares that in the incarnation of Christ—His dwelling among human beings—'we beheld His glory, glory as of the only begotten from the Father, full of grace and truth' (John 1:14). How was His glory manifested on earth? Through His words and His works. His first miracle at the wedding in Cana served to display His glory (John 2:1-11), followed by every miracle thereafter. But He did not live to glorify Himself: 'I do not seek My own glory' (John 8:50); for He said, 'If I glorify Myself, My glory is nothing;

it is My Father who glorifies Me' (v. 54). In the end, Christ declared that He came to glorify the Father on earth (John 17:4) — to put on display the power, wisdom, holiness, and majesty of our great God. Before His death, Jesus cried out, 'Father, glorify Your name,' to which He responded from heaven, 'I have both glorified it, and will glorify it again' (John 12:28).

Perhaps one of the most dynamic expressions of the glory of Christ comes in Matthew 17 on the Mountain of Transfiguration. Jesus brings Peter, James, and John up to the top of the mountain, and transfigures before them, 'His face shone like the sun, and His garments became as white as light' (Matt. 17:2 NASB). No doubt a preview of His future glory (Rev. 1:13-16), this earthly glimpse puts on display the majestic brilliance of Jesus Christ as the Son of God, the Second Person of the Trinity in all His power and deity. He is the object of our hope, as we look forward to 'the appearing of the glory of our great God and Savior, Christ Jesus' (Titus 2:13)

Beyond beholding the intrinsic glory of God, and ascribing to Him all glory, there is a part for the church to play.

For the Sake of God's Glory

Every human being who has ever existed has sinned against God and fallen short of His glory (Rom. 3:23). However, the redemption of believers through the blood of Jesus Christ is not merely unto idleness. We weren't just saved to sit. Rather, we have a blessed work to do; a role to play in the story of redemption. Once we are saved—justified; we are called to be sanctified—to become conformed to the image of the Son (Rom. 8:29), who is called 'the Lord of glory' (1 Cor. 2:8).

Writing to the church, the apostle Paul reminds them of the ramifications of their salvation: 'For you have been bought with a price,' referring to the ransoming work of Christ, 'therefore glorify God in your body' (1 Cor. 6:20 NASB). More than simply acknowledging and *ascribing* glory to God, we are called to live in such a way that honors Him and makes beautiful His righteous reputation on earth. Jesus told the disciples, 'Let your light shine before men in such a way that they may see your good works, and glorify your Father who is in heaven' (Matt. 5:16 NASB). Not only are we called to glorify God, we are called to give cause for *others* to glorify God!

In the event of our salvation—our election, redemption, sealing, etc.—God was doing all things 'to the praise of His glory" (Eph. 1:6, 12, 14). As we live our lives, Peter writes, 'in all things God may be glorified through Jesus Christ, to whom belongs the glory and dominion forever and ever' (1 Pet. 4:11 NASB). Even in persecution and suffering, we are not to feel ashamed, but 'in the [name of Christ] let [us] glorify God' (v. 16). In fact, the manner of Peter's death, Jesus told him, would glorify God (John 21:19). In all aspects of life—our marriages and family, our professions and hobbies, in prosperity and pain, in joy and sorrow; everything exists for God's glory. Paul concludes, 'Whether, then, you eat or drink or whatever you do, do all to the glory of God' (1 Cor. 10:31 NASB).

The Bible is clear. God is a God of glory. The Lord Jesus Christ is the incarnation of His glory. The Spirit empowers believers to live to give Him glory. Further, we know that 'All nations whom [God] has made shall come and worship before [Him]... and they shall glorify [His] name' (Ps. 86:9 NASB).

How did the Reformers understand and obey the command to glorify God?

The Glory of God in the Reformation

The Reformers knew that they needed to surrender to God more than just their professions of faith. They knew that their faith needed to have arms and legs—to reach beyond theory. In obedience to this mandate, they sought to reform all areas of life.

As we've seen, they reformed their *Doctrine*. More than simply the five *solas*, men like Martin Luther, Philip Melanchthon, and John Calvin labored tirelessly to study the Scriptures, and re-establish a body of teaching for the benefit of Christians worldwide.

They reformed *The Church*. Christendom had been held captive to the religious burdens of the Roman Catholic Church for a thousand years, but the Reformers protested the unbiblical practices and ungodly behaviors of the priests, and sought to establish the bounds of a true church—those who had been converted through saving faith in Jesus Christ. Further, worship gatherings were modified to better reflect what was seen in the New Testament.

They reformed *Marriage and Family*. Europe in the Middle Ages maintained a low view of marriage, seeing the institution more in terms of practical functionality, and less about a loving relationship. Subsequently, children were de-valued and derided. Because of their love for God—loving what He loves—Protestants elevated marriage and valued their children.

They reformed *Education*. At a time when learning was reserved only for the elite, Protestants worked tirelessly to provide quality broad-based education for people of all ages and social classes. One of the markers of Protestantism in the first 300 years of its existence was the aggressive effort to establish institutions of learning. From Wittenberg and Geneva to Great Britain and New England, education has been a hallmark of the Reformation.

They reformed *Society*. Not a single aspect of culture was left untouched—work and vocation, the arts, leisure, economics, industry, even the fight for human rights; all of society was subject to the Protestant effort. They erased the sacred-secular divide, insisting that every activity could be done for the glory of God.

Finally, they reformed *Government*. Ever since Pope Leo III crowned Charlemagne as king of the Holy Roman Empire in A.D. 800, the Catholic Church has asserted itself as a supreme authority in matters of religion and government. But the Protestant Reformation challenged that authority, seeking not to elevate earthly rulers to a higher place than directed by Scripture. Commenting on this ideal, New England pastor John Cotton said:

'Let all the world learn to give mortal men no greater power than they are content they shall use, for use it they will ... It is necessary therefore, that all power that is on earth be limited.'[14]

While the Reformers and their descendants were happy to submit themselves to governing authorities (Rom. 13:1-7; Titus 3:1-2), they rejected the notion that government had the right to take the place of God over the lives of people.

For the Glory of God Alone

Over and above all else, the Reformation was an effort to move religion away from a man-centered scheme of self-justification and self-salvation to the God-glorifying, Christ-centered, Spirit-empowered religion of the Scriptures. John Calvin maintained, 'We never truly glory in [God] until we have utterly discarded our own glory ... The elect are justified by the Lord, in order that they may glory in him, and in none else.'[15]

But the Reformers realized that this battle would need to be fought in every generation. As soon as we begin to rest on our laurels, complacency and pride overtake us, and we find ourselves sinfully trusting in our own efforts again. That's why we must be committed to *semper reformanda*—to be 'always reforming.'

The Puritans were the spiritual descendants of the Reformers in England, and in the 1640s, they met together and drafted a declaration of their unified belief and doctrine, known as The Westminster Confession of Faith. In teaching this confession to the church, they established *catechisms*—a series of questions and answers to help solidify biblical doctrine into the hearts and minds of believers. Question 1 asks, 'What is the chief end of man?' In the spirit of *soli Deo gloria*, the answer is given: 'Man's chief end is

---

14. Quoted in Terry L. Johnson, *The Case for Traditional Protestantism: The Solas of the Reformation* (Edinburgh: Banner of Truth Trust, 2004), 155.

15. David Vandrunen, *God's Glory Alone: The Majestic Heart of Christian Faith and Life* (Grand Rapids: Zondervan, 2015), 13.

to glorify God, and to enjoy him forever.' From the Puritans all the way back to the Apostles, Christians have understood and believed that glorifying God has always been their primary task.

However, if we deny *sola Scriptura*, we effectively make our own wisdom and experience the authority in all spiritual life, and not the revealed Word of God. If we deny *sola gratia*, we elevate our own will above the sovereign will of God. If we deny *sola fide*, we exalt our own self-righteous works, while diminishing the saving work of Jesus Christ. If we deny *solus Christus*, we fix our gaze on created beings, and not on Christ, as the object of our worship and adoration. A denial of biblical Christian doctrine makes us idolaters, and robs God of the glory due His name. However, if we live and believe in such a way that glorifies the Lord, then all of our Christian life exists *soli Deo gloria*—for the glory of God alone.

'For from Him and through Him and to Him are all things. To Him be the glory forever. Amen' (Rom. 11:36).

Come now, let us reason together ...
(Isaiah 1:18)

A Final Word

Let me be as honest as I can: my earnest prayer is that every person would recognize their own need of salvation, repent and confess their sin to God, trust in the Lord Jesus Christ, and find life in His name. The Scriptures tell us that 'there is salvation in no one else; for there is no other name under heaven given among men, by which we must be saved' (Acts 4:12). Jesus declared, 'I am the way, and the truth, and the life; no one comes to the Father except through Me' (John 14:6). He is the only way of salvation.

However, there are many faith systems that claim the name of Jesus, yet deny what He teaches; they deny the gospel as laid out in the Bible. One of the greatest deceptions put forth by Satan is the propagation of *almost* Christianity—a Christianity that looks and sounds like the real thing, but that is completely antithetical to biblical Christianity. And although Roman Catholicism uses many of the same words, phrases, and Scriptures, as we've seen, it does not ultimately lead people in the way of salvation.

I have a deep love for *devout Catholics*, as they have a sincere desire to know Jesus Christ! However, do they know the true Christ—the Christ of the Bible? The question needs to be asked: Does Roman Catholic dogma align with Scripture or are there contradictions? Remember, there were no 'Protestants' in 1517;

only Christians who cared enough about their faith to test all things against the Word of God. Let us be like the noble Bereans in Acts 17:11 and examine everything in light of what God has revealed in the Holy Bible. Jesus said, 'It is finished!' The Christian life is lived in humble obedience and worship to the Lord for what He has already accomplished, and not in fear of ourselves not doing enough.

I have hope for those who are *religious,' yet uncommitted*. When the apostle Paul stood before those who were 'seeking' for God, he affirmed that many 'seek [for] God, if perhaps they might grope for Him and find Him, though He is not far from each one of us; for in Him we live and move and exist' (Acts 17:27-28 NASB). People usually go to church or read religious books because of something deep inside them that tells them they should. However, it is God who has implanted an innate sense of Him in the heart (Rom. 1:19-21; 2:14-15)! But God can be known through what He has revealed to us in the Bible—that Jesus is God in human flesh, the Savior of the world, and the only hope for eternal life.

I praise God for *Protestants*!—those who have accepted the Bible as the Word of God and salvation by God's grace alone through faith alone in Jesus Christ alone. But let us not be like the Ephesians who forgot their first love (Rev. 2:4), or the Laodiceans who let themselves become lukewarm to the things of God (Rev. 3:15-16). Believers should always strive to deepen their *love* and *knowledge* of God, and never to let their light grow dim (Matt. 5:15).

In the end, this is not about the Five *Solas*, or even the Protestant Reformation. It's about the glory of God and the gospel of Jesus Christ. It's about recovering and contending for authentic Christianity. It's about communicating a saving gospel to all the world—that Jesus Christ came and died on the cross to save sinners.

'Now I make known to you, brethren, the gospel which I preached to you, which also you received, in which also you stand, by which also you are saved, if you hold fast the word which I preached to you, unless you believed in vain. For I delivered to you as of first importance what I also received, that Christ died for our sins according to the Scriptures, and that He was buried, and that He was raised on the third day according to the Scriptures.' (1 Cor. 15:1-4 NASB)

May the truth of the gospel be proclaimed in every corner of the world, and the name of Jesus Christ lifted up to the highest heaven! May He receive all honor and worship and praise!

Soli Deo Gloria!

Appendix 1
The Priesthood of All Believers

So far in this book, we have explored the five *solas* of the Reformation: *sola Scriptura, sola gratia, sola fide, solus Christus,* and *soli Deo gloria.* In doing so, we noted that the main thrust of the Reformation was a recovery of the Christian understanding that salvation was by God's grace alone through faith alone in Christ alone, for the glory of God alone, based on the authority of Scripture alone.

While the *solas* were not official decrees made by the Reformers themselves, we understand that they provide a basic framework for understanding what was at stake for them. They believed that the Roman Catholic Church, over the course of one thousand years, had wandered away from biblical Christianity. Therefore, out of love for Christ and His church, the Reformers labored to rescue it and to reform it.

However, their labors were not limited to the broad area of the five *solas.* Numerous elements were touched on in the writings of Martin Luther, Philip Melanchthon, John Calvin, and others. There were other key themes of the Reformation. And for our purposes, we will explore three of them, beginning with 'The Priesthood of All Believers.'

Luther on Abuses

The year 1520 was an important year in the life of the early Reformation. Martin Luther, only three years earlier, on October 31, 1517, had nailed his 95 Theses to the church door in Wittenberg, Germany. These were 95 points of contention with the Roman Catholic Church—95 protests, if you will. But in the years that followed, Luther began to expound on those various points of contention—writing voraciously and exhaustively.

In 1520, three key treatises were published: *To the Christian Nobility of the German Nation*, *The Babylonian Captivity of the Church*, and *The Freedom of a Christian*. In the first treatise, *To the Christian Nobility*, Luther attacked the corrupt power structure of the Roman Catholic Church, particularly the papacy. His argument was that the Popes and Catholic leaders had used their power and influence to oppress and abuse the people underneath them. And these abuses were made possible by a complex theological fortress that had to be torn down in order to be exposed and remedied.

In the opening section of his treatise, Luther addresses what he refers to as 'three walls' behind which the papacy was entrenched. Luther believed that these three strongholds needed to be exposed in order to uproot the ungodly papacy.

The first wall had to do with the separation of the clergy and the laity. This wall was built on the notion of two realms—the clergy occupying the spiritual realm, while the laity were of the temporal realm.

The second wall was built on the notion that only the Pope could truly understand the Scriptures, therefore, he could not be challenged.

The third wall was a reinforcement of the second wall; even if you wanted to form a council to oppose the Pope, only the Pope himself was permitted to summon a council. Therefore, opposing the Pope was impossible.

But Luther understood that before he could address the Pope directly, he had to first deal with the issue of the clergy-laity distinction. He writes, 'It is pure invention that Pope, bishop, priests, and monks are called the spiritual estate while princes, lords, artisans, and farmers are called the temporal estate.'[1] In other words, regular church-people (laity) were viewed as inferior and less spiritual than the religious leaders, known as 'clergy.' Popes and priests were seen as super-Christians who were closer to God, while the rest were all 'commoners,' looking to the spiritual class for help, blessing, and guidance.

But Luther said, 'This is indeed a piece of deceit and hypocrisy… all Christians are truly of the spiritual estates, and there is no difference among them except that of office.'[2] At that point, Luther cites the words of the apostle Paul in 1 Corinthians 12:12-13, that 'we are all one body.' He continues, 'The Pope or bishop anoints, shaves heads, ordains, consecrates, and prescribes garb different from that of the laity, but he can never make a man into a Christian or into a spiritual man by doing so … a hypocrite or a humbug and blockhead, but never a Christian or a spiritual man.'[3]

Once believers understood that they were not second-class Christians, the Reformation began to pick up speed. Luther and others taught that there wasn't a ruling class of spiritual priestly elite, but rather, the church consisted of a different priesthood—the priesthood of *all* believers. This notion was derived from the primary text of Scripture, namely 1 Peter 2.

A Royal Priesthood

First Peter is a letter to the dispersed church—those who are living in times of great persecution. The letter opens with Peter reminding the church of their hope in Christ. He tells them, '[God] has caused us to be born again to a living hope through the resurrection of Jesus Christ from the dead' (1 Pet. 1:3). The reality of our salvation

---

1. Martin Luther, *To the Christian Nobility of the German Nation* in *Three Treatises* (Minneapolis: Fortress Press, 1970), 12.

2. ibid.

3. ibid.

should produce joy and thanksgiving. However, our salvation is not a cause for spiritual lethargy. Rather, he reminds them of the command of God to be holy. He tells them to 'be sober-minded' (v. 13) and 'be obedient' (v. 14)—positive encouragements.

Then he opens up chapter two with admonitions—'put away all malice and all deceit and hypocrisy and envy and all slander' (2:1). These are calls to holiness. But all of this is not merely disjointed commands for obedience. Rather, he explains the reason why their holiness is so important:

> As you come to him, a living stone rejected by men but in the sight of God chosen and precious, you yourselves like living stones are being built up as a spiritual house, to be a holy priesthood, to offer spiritual sacrifices acceptable to God through Jesus Christ. For it stands in Scripture: 'Behold, I am laying in Zion a stone, a cornerstone chosen and precious, and whoever believes in him will not be put to shame.' So the honor is for you who believe, but for those who do not believe, 'The stone that the builders rejected has become the cornerstone,' and 'A stone of stumbling, and a rock of offense.' They stumble because they disobey the word, as they were destined to do. But you are a chosen race, a royal priesthood, a holy nation, a people for his own possession, that you may proclaim the excellencies of him who called you out of darkness into his marvelous light. Once you were not a people, but now you are God's people; once you had not received mercy, but now you have received mercy (1 Peter 2:4-10).

In this passage, Peter refers to the body of Christ by several different names. In verse 5, he refers to believers as 'living stones,' which are used as building materials comprising 'a spiritual house.' Twice in the passage, the church is called a 'priesthood'—'a *holy* priesthood' (v. 5) and 'a *royal* priesthood' (v. 9). Also, in verse 9, the church is called 'a chosen race,' 'a holy nation,' and 'a people for [God's] own possession.' For our purposes, let's examine the church as a *priesthood*.

In the Old Testament, the priest functioned as a mediator between God and man. We read about how God appointed a whole line of priests from the tribe of Levi. And it was set up specifically through Moses's brother, Aaron, and his sons—Aaron being appointed as the first 'high priest.' What was known as the 'Levitical' or 'Aaronic' priesthood (named for Aaron) would have special duties to facilitate the worship of God in Israel.

One of their primary duties was to offer sacrifices to God on behalf of the people. We see the types of sacrifices in the first seven chapters of Leviticus. And the way this would work is, when a person would sin, they would select out a spotless lamb (or a bull or goat), bring it to the temple, confess their sins to the Lord, and the priest would help them slaughter the animal, and offer it up on the altar. After all, we understand from the explanation given in Hebrews 9:22, 'almost everything was purified with blood, and without the shedding of blood, there is no forgiveness of sins.' So, the priest would help the worshiper repent and offer sacrifices for sins.

Now the requirements for the priest were many. They had to be descended from the right tribe, of the right lineage. They had to be consecrated for the work; be devout and meticulous in their labor. They had to be ceremonially clean, morally pure, upright and holy unto the Lord. But they were really only meant to serve as examples for all of Israel. After all, in Exodus 19, back when the Lord brought Israel out of bondage, He told them that *all* of Israel would serve Him as 'a kingdom of priests and a holy nation' (v. 6).

God's true desire was for *all* of His people to be consecrated, devout, pure, and holy. But, if God desired all of Israel to function as priests, then why did He create a Levitical system? The answer was, to show them the extreme wickedness of sin, and their desperate need for a Savior.

Christ as High Priest

At the heart of Hebrews, Jesus is put on display as the ultimate fulfillment of the sacrificial system. Hebrews 4:15 tells us that Jesus, as our great high priest, sympathizes with our weaknesses; that He was tempted like us yet never once sinned. And Jesus, although He is not from the tribe of Levi, but of Judah, is a rightful high priest because He comes through a higher order—not from Levi, but His priesthood comes through the order of Melchizedek.

We read about Melchizedek the priest in Genesis 14, and how Abraham pays tithes to him, acknowledging the existence of an eternal priesthood that existed before Levi was even born. Christ is of that *eternal* priesthood according to Hebrews 7. But we learn that the entire sacrificial system served as a copy and shadow of a greater spiritual reality. And that, in truth, the blood of bulls and goats never took away sin; they only pointed to the reality that Christ needed to come and die. We read:

> But when Christ appeared as a high priest of the good things that have come, then through the greater and more perfect tent (not made with hands, that is, not of this creation) he entered once for all into the holy places, not by means of the blood of goats and calves but by means of his own blood, thus securing an eternal redemption. For if the blood of goats and bulls, and the sprinkling of defiled persons with the ashes of a heifer, sanctify for the purification of the flesh, how much more will the blood of Christ, who through the eternal Spirit offered himself without blemish to God, purify our conscience from dead works to serve the living God. Therefore he is the mediator of a new covenant, so that those who are called may receive the promised eternal inheritance, since a death has occurred that redeems them from the transgressions committed under the first covenant (Heb. 9:11-15).

Furthermore, we read:

> For Christ has entered, not into holy places made with hands, which are copies of the true things, but into heaven itself, now to appear in the presence of God on our behalf. Nor was it to offer himself repeatedly, as the high priest enters the holy places every

year with blood not his own, for then he would have had to suffer repeatedly since the foundation of the world. But as it is, he has appeared once for all at the end of the ages to put away sin by the sacrifice of himself. And just as it is appointed for man to die once, and after that comes judgment, so Christ, having been offered once to bear the sins of many, will appear a second time, not to deal with sin but to save those who are eagerly waiting for him (vv. 24-28).

When Jesus Christ died on the cross, the veil in the temple was torn from top to bottom. The Levitical priesthood was ended; the sacrificial system was obliterated. No longer do worshipers of God need to offer sacrifices on an altar. No longer do you need to go to a human priest to make your confession. No longer is God's wrath only *temporarily* satisfied; for Romans 8:1 tells us that 'there is therefore now no condemnation for those who are in Christ Jesus.'

In other words, if Christ Jesus is your high priest, and if He is your sacrifice for sin, and if He is your atonement, then you don't need any more sacrifices and you don't need any priests. So, why then does God desire a new covenant priesthood? We find our answer again in our 1 Peter text.

Offering Spiritual Sacrifices

Whereas, in the old covenant, worship was offered to God through the ministry of the priesthood, God still wants worshipers. In fact, Jesus said in John 4:23–24, that 'the Father is seeking such people to worship him ... those who worship him ... in spirit and truth.' He told Israel that His endgame was to have a 'holy nation,' a 'kingdom of priests.' He now has it in the Bride of Christ.

In 1 Peter 2:5 he tells the believers that, like stones in a building, they are 'living stones.' They are being built up into 'a royal priesthood.' What is our role as a kingdom of priests? It is 'to offer spiritual sacrifices acceptable to God through Jesus Christ' (v. 5). He is already our sacrifice—the Lamb of God who takes away the sins of the world (cf. John 1:29, 36). He is also our high priest who acts as the mediator between God and man (cf. 1 Tim. 2:5).

We don't offer blood sacrifices or earthly sacrifices. Instead, we offer spiritual sacrifices. We submit the offerings of praise, worship, and dedication. Philippians 2:17 calls our faith a sacrificial offering. 1 Peter 4:10 tells us that each of us receive gifts from the Lord. We see examples of spiritual gifts such as preaching, teaching, serving, giving, administration, helps, wisdom, encouragement, leadership, mercy, and so on, listed in 1 Corinthians 12 and Romans 12. Peter notes, 'as each has received a gift, use it to serve one another' (1 Pet. 4:10). And when we use our gifts to serve others, according to Philippians 4:18, such gifts are seen as 'a fragrant offering, a sacrifice acceptable and pleasing to God.'

If you try and give a spiritual gift without offering it through Christ—in other words, in order to improve your own standing before God—it's wasted! The offering is only acceptable to God through the ministry and mediation of our great high priest, Jesus Christ.

What other offerings do we bring? Romans 12:1-2 says that we offer our bodies and our minds to God as 'living sacrifices.' We read in Matthew 10:39 that we are to 'lose [our] life' in order to find it. Yes, Jesus said that we are even to offer up our whole selves! Again, not that making these spiritual offerings gets us saved or scores points with God! No, they are free-will offerings of praise, worship, adoration, and obedience. One Peter 2:9 says that we are 'a royal priesthood ... a people for his own possession, that you may proclaim the excellencies of him who called you out of darkness and into his marvelous light.' As priests of the new covenant, operating under the ministry of Christ, the great high priest, we have been called, equipped, and sent to proclaim the excellencies of Christ. Gregg Allison notes,

As heir of the Protestant doctrine of the priesthood of all believers, evangelical theology encourages all Christians to engage in intercessory prayer for each other, hear others' confession of sin and assure those penitents of God's forgiveness, engage missionally together for the cause of Christ, teach and admonish one another with the Word of God (Col. 3:16), and much more.[4]

We proclaim the gospel. We teach doctrine. We share the good news. We love one another. We bear one another's burdens. And we do it all in full reverence of, and in service to, Jesus Christ. This is nothing short of New Covenant priestly service. 'The Priesthood of All Believers' is the reality that every man is a minister; every woman is a minister. There is no spiritual elite. There is no exclusive priesthood, those who have accepted 'holy orders.' There is only the priesthood of all believers, with Christ Jesus as our great high priest and chief cornerstone.

---

4.   Gregg R. Allison, *Roman Catholic Theology & Practice: An Evangelical Assessment* (Wheaton: Crossway, 2014), 369.

Appendix 2
Theology of the Cross

In his book, *Reformation: Yesterday, Today and Tomorrow*, Carl Trueman noted that one topic 'takes us very close to the heart of... Reformation theology.'[1] He notes further, 'The Reformation was ... a supremely Christ-centered movement ... and no one theologian expressed this Christ-saturated approach more dramatically than Martin Luther in his theology of the cross.'[2] However, before we get too far ahead of ourselves, let's first take a look at Luther's own struggle before discovering the cross.

Luther's Lament

Growing up in a normal German Catholic home, Luther was exposed to everything the Church of Rome taught. His mother was very devout and superstitious, and sowed into him many deeply-held fears: the fear of hell and the fear of judgment. All his life he felt like God was stalking him, looking for reasons to strike him down.

His view of Christ was based on many of the painted Medieval murals, one in particular—a painting of Jesus sitting on a rainbow,

---

1. Carl R. Trueman, *Reformation: Yesterday, Today and Tomorrow* (Fearn, Ross-shire: Christian Focus, 2012), 44.
2. ibid., 45.

holding seven stars in His hand, and a sword of judgment protruding from His mouth. This terrifying vision of the judgment of Christ weighed heavily on Luther, and would later compel him to join a monastery, dedicating his life to the service of the church.[3]

But all his life, God was a mystery to him. And the common belief by many in his day was that God could not be truly known. This led many to speculation and philosophy, and left churchgoers without hope. By Luther's own recollection, he didn't even see a Bible until he was twenty years old. He lived in fear of the unknown.

But after being sent to Wittenberg to teach theology, Luther began to work through the Bible—some of the texts for the very first time. On August 1, 1513 he began his study in the Psalms. It would be his studies of Paul's letters to the Galatians and to the Romans that would lead him into his own personal discovery of the doctrine of justification. But it would be his studies in Psalm 22 that would point him to Christ.

The Suffering Savior's Cross

Psalms 22, 23 and 24 form a thematic unit. Psalm 24 is speaking about the Lord, the King of glory. Psalm 23 portrays the Lord as our Shepherd. But Psalm 22 is a psalm of trouble, pain, and loneliness. Written by David to address his own pain and struggle, as well as his feelings of abandonment by the Lord, the New Testament records Jesus using many of these words, some of them even on the cross.

Both Matthew 27 and Mark 15 record Jesus crying out, 'My God, My God, why have you forsaken me?' This is a direct quote from Psalm 22:1. Furthermore, verses 14 through 18 describe vividly the suffering experienced by Jesus at His crucifixion.

> I am poured out like water, and all my bones are out of joint; my
> heart is like wax; it is melted within my breast; my strength is dried
> up like a potsherd, and my tongue sticks to my jaws; you lay me in

---

3. Roland H. Bainton, *Here I Stand: A Life of Martin Luther* (Peabody: Hendrickson, 1977), 10-11.

the dust of death. For dogs encompass me; a company of evildoers encircles me; they have pierced my hands and feet—I can count all my bones—they stare and gloat over me; they divide my garments among them, and for my clothing they cast lots (Ps. 22:14-18).

Upon reading this passage, suddenly Luther's view of Christ began to change. The image of Christ was *not* that of Judge. Rather, it was the image of Christ as sufferer, as the Man of Sorrows. Luther's biographer, Roland Bainton notes:

> The utter desolation which Luther said he could not endure ... had been experienced by Christ himself as he died. Rejected of men, he was rejected also of God ... Christ had suffered what Luther suffered, or rather Luther was finding himself in what Christ had suffered ...
>
> Why should Christ have known such desperations? Luther knew perfectly well why he himself had had them: he was weak in the presence of the Mighty; he was impure in the presence of the Holy; he had blasphemed the Divine Majesty. But Christ was not weak; Christ was not impure; Christ was not impious. Why then should he have been so overwhelmed with desolation? The only answer must be that Christ took to himself the iniquity of us all. He who was without sin for our sakes became sin and so identified himself with us as to participate in our alienation.[4]

God is still holy. God is still Judge. But He is also Savior and Redeemer. And through this display, Luther came to see that the intersection of all the holiness and righteousness and justice of God and the sinfulness and wretchedness of sinful man—all of it came to a head at the cross of Jesus Christ.

The Theology of Glory

Luther alluded to his Psalm 22 discovery in his *95 Theses*, having posted them in Wittenberg on October 31, 1517. But he would

---

4. Roland H. Bainton, *Here I Stand: A Life of Martin Luther* (Peabody: Hendrickson, 1977), 44-45.

explore the idea more in the following years. In 1518 he was given the opportunity to explain his views in what came to be known as the Heidelberg Disputation. It was there that he made note of two distinct views: *the theology of glory* versus *the theology of the cross.* Keeping in mind that the big theological question of Luther's day (and even for our day) is: Can God be truly known? And, if so, how?

The church of Rome at the time was filled with theologians who engaged in philosophical speculation. How are we to know a God who is invisible? they would posit. The 'theologians of glory,' as Luther called them, relied on their own wisdom and experience to answer such questions. They valued mysticism and deep pondering. They believed that by the best efforts of the wisest, most spiritual, most learned men, they could figure out how to best know God. Carl Trueman and Eunjin Kim note:

> [*T*]*he theologian of glory* assumes that God is made in man's image and thus conforms to human expectations. So, for example, to please God, one does good works to earn his favor, as one would do with a fellow human being.[5]

But the Bible says, as Luther noted, that our righteous deeds are filthy rags before God (Isa. 64:6). And when done apart from God's grace are nothing more than an exercise in self-righteousness.

In fact, we even hear about this today—people trying to conform God into *their* image, making up their own rules and expecting God to obey them. I remember attending a funeral at a Roman Catholic Church and hearing the priest say, over and over, 'All God expects is that we do the best that we can.' Probably half a dozen times, he reiterated, 'We're not perfect; God can't expect us to be perfect. But He wants us to do the best that we can.'

---

5. Carl R. Trueman and Eunjin Kim, 'The Reformers and Their Reformations' in *Reformation Theology: A Systematic Summary*, Matthew Barrett, ed. (Wheaton: Crossway, 2017), 113.

However, Matthew 5:48 commands us, 'You therefore must be perfect, as your heavenly Father is perfect.' To this the listener must admit, 'I cannot be perfect!' And if so, then you must die, because 'the wages of sin is death' (Rom. 6:23). God is not asking us for 'the best that we can.' That's a made-up idea, concocted in the minds of so-called 'theologians of glory'—the idea that our relationship with God is founded in *our* ability to be good. If you live like that, you will no doubt perish! On this, Luther writes, 'A theologian of glory calls evil good and good evil. A theologian of the cross calls the thing what it actually is.'[6]

So, what is *the theology of the cross*?

The Theology of the Cross

First, it is an answer to the question, Can God be known? And the answer is yes, but not by speculation, imagination, or reason. Instead, we know God by *revelation*. God has chosen to reveal Himself to His people. He has told us things. He has shown us things. And the most poignant revelation was that of His Son, Jesus Christ. And in revealing the Son, there was no event more crucial, more central, more real than the event of the cross. This was why Paul maintained in 1 Corinthians 2:2, 'For I decided to know nothing among you except Jesus Christ and Him crucified.' It's the pinnacle expression of God's revelation—the saving work of Jesus on the cross.

After telling Nicodemus about the need to be born again in John 3, Jesus made note of a truth concealed yet now revealed: 'As Moses lifted up the serpent in the wilderness, so must the Son of Man be lifted up, that whoever believes in Him may have eternal life' (John 3:14-15). And what is eternal life? We read in John 17:3, 'And this is eternal life, that they may know...the only true God, and Jesus Christ whom [He] has sent.' The only way anyone can know

---

6.   Cited in Donald Macleod, 'The Work of Christ' in *Reformation Theology: A Systematic Summary*, Matthew Barrett, ed. (Wheaton: Crossway, 2017), 386.

God and experience eternal life is by believing on the crucified Son of God.

But how do we know God through the cross of Christ?

1. We see the love of God in the Cross

In John 3:16 we read, 'For God so loved the world, He gave His only begotten Son, that whosoever believes in Him should not perish but have everlasting life.' The mere fact that the Son of God even came to earth to die for us is a demonstration of God's love— that He would love people so much that He would descend from heaven, take on a human body, be abused and tortured, and then die, surrounded by those who mock and ridicule Him, is nothing short of pure love. Romans 5:8 declares to us, 'For God demonstrates His own love for us, in that, while we were still sinners, Christ died for us.' The cross of Christ was the single greatest act of God's love toward us.

2. We see the justice of God against wickedness

The apostle Paul explains in Romans chapter 3:

> But now the righteousness of God has been manifested apart from the law, although the Law and the Prophets bear witness to it—the righteousness of God through faith in Jesus Christ for all who believe. For there is no distinction: for all have sinned and fall short of the glory of God, and are justified by his grace as a gift, through the redemption that is in Christ Jesus, whom God put forward as a propitiation by his blood, to be received by faith. This was to show God's righteousness, because in his divine forbearance he had passed over former sins. It was to show his righteousness at the present time, so that he might be just and the justifier of the one who has faith in Jesus (vv. 21-26).

In the death of Christ, God upholds His own justice by punishing *all* sin, *all* unrighteousness, and *all* iniquity. He pours out the full cup on His own wrath, but does so on the *one* person in history who doesn't deserve it! But God's justice was served in the death of Christ. His righteousness was upheld, His holiness preserved, and His glory displayed. But no one can look at the suffering death of Jesus and *not* feel the heat of God's wrath. After all, who doesn't tremble at the voice of Jesus crying out, 'My God, my God, why have you forsaken me?' The weight of punishment is revealed at the cross.

3. *We also see the mercy of God in the Cross*

While the theology of glory dares to say, 'Do the best that you can ...' the theology of the cross recognizes, 'I can't—Oh wretched man that I am!' It asks, 'God, will you show mercy on me, the sinner?' And God is able to show mercy because of the cross. It is mercy that 'He made Him to be sin who knew no sin, so that in Him we might become the righteousness of God' (2 Cor. 5:21). We, who were far off, were brought near because of the cross of Christ.

Now, all of these things we *know* to be true, because God tells us they're true. However, Luther's *theology of the cross* goes a bit further. Luther believed and taught that God is also made known to us through suffering. To think, Christ was never more human to us than when He was at the height of His suffering on the cross. Physically, the nails had pierced His hands and feet, the thorns digging into His head, even His back aching from the whips. David records the scene prophetically in Psalm 22:

> 'all my bones are out of joint'
> 'my heart is like wax'
> 'my strength is dried up'
> 'my tongue sticks to my jaws'
> 'my hands and feet are pierced'
> 'I can count all my bones'

This was the height of physical pain. But there's also the mental, emotional, and spiritual suffering of being betrayed by friends, feeling totally alone, even being forsaken by His own Father. Yes,

Jesus is intimately acquainted with human suffering. For we read, 'For we do not have a high priest who is unable to sympathize with our weaknesses' (Heb. 4:15). And He, too, was tempted, yet without any sin.

But in the suffering of Jesus, He identified with us. And so, in our suffering, we identify with Him. In fact, as Christians, we have a portion of suffering marked out for us. Consider the following: 'Because you are not of the world, the world hates you' (John 15:19), 'In this life, you will have tribulation'—suffering—'but take heart, I have overcome the world' (John 16:33), or the words of Paul who preached to the saints in Lystra, 'Strengthening [their] souls, encouraging [them] to continue in the faith, and saying that through many tribulations we must enter the kingdom of God' (Acts 14:22).

So, we're going to struggle in this life. It will be hard. We will experience a measure of suffering. But God desires that we embrace it, looking for opportunities to draw closer to Him.

Suffering Well

One of the key themes in First Peter is that of suffering well. And one might ask, what enables us to do that? The answer is, 'the true grace of God' (1 Pet. 5:12). But chapter 4 gives us a very raw look at suffering in the Christian life. We read:

> Since therefore Christ suffered in the flesh, arm yourselves with the same way of thinking, for whoever has suffered in the flesh has ceased from sin, so as to live for the rest of the time in the flesh no longer for human passions but for the will of God (1 Pet. 4:1-2).

So, he directs their thinking by saying, 'Have a right view of suffering.' Jesus didn't run away from it. Rather He submitted Himself to the will of God. And so should we. But then, in verses 12 through 19, Peter gives us some help. We read:

Beloved, do not be surprised at the fiery trial when it comes upon you to test you, as though something strange were happening to you. But rejoice insofar as you share Christ's sufferings, that you may also rejoice and be glad when his glory is revealed. If you are insulted for the name of Christ, you are blessed, because the Spirit of glory and of God rests upon you. But let none of you suffer as a murderer or a thief or an evildoer or as a meddler. Yet if anyone suffers as a Christian, let him not be ashamed, but let him glorify God in that name. For it is time for judgment to begin at the household of God; and if it begins with us, what will be the outcome for those who do not obey the gospel of God? And 'If the righteous is scarcely saved, what will become of the ungodly and the sinner?' Therefore let those who suffer according to God's will entrust their souls to a faithful Creator while doing good (1 Pet. 4:12-19).

In this passage, we see a few of God's purposes for our suffering:

First, *suffering exists to test us*. Peter explicitly says this in verse 12: 'do not be surprised at the fiery trial when it comes upon you to test you.' When trials come, don't be surprised! Recognize that they are God's tool for testing and growing you. In fact, James 1:2 tells us that trials are for the testing of our faith in order to produce endurance in us. And so, suffering is for our testing.

Second, *suffering produces joy*. This may seem like an odd notion at first, but when we look at verse 13 we read, 'But rejoice insofar as you share Christ's sufferings, that you may also rejoice and be glad when his glory is revealed.' In the moment, trials are often unpleasant and difficult. But if you were to ask any Christian who has persevered by faith, when they come out the other side, they are filled with joy because they see God's hand in the midst of their suffering. And so we ask, How much *more* joy will we have when God's glory is finally revealed?

Third, *suffering produces blessing*. We read in verse 14, 'If you are insulted for the name of Christ, you are blessed, because the

Spirit of glory and of God rests upon you.' In this context, Peter is pointing to persecution—when others harass you for being a Christian. But when you keep your testimony and persevere in your trial, God blesses you.

Fourth, *suffering is cause for worship*. Note what Peter says in verses 15 and 16: 'But let none of you suffer as a murderer or a thief or an evildoer or as a meddler. Yet if anyone suffers as a Christian, let him not be ashamed, but let him glorify God in that name.' The context here is a person who suffers, not for doing something wrong, but for doing something right. More specifically, for living as a Christian. Again, if you keep your testimony, he says, 'don't be ashamed, but glorify God!' The disciples in Acts 5 rejoiced and praised God when they were whipped by the Jewish leaders of the Sanhedrin. They rejoiced that they were 'counted worthy to suffer dishonor for Christ's name' (v. 41).

Fifth, *suffering chastens us*. We see in verses 17 and 18, 'For it is time for judgment to begin at the household of God; and if it begins with us, what will be the outcome for those who do not obey the gospel of God? And "If the righteous is scarcely saved, what will become of the ungodly and the sinner?"' God disciplines those He loves (cf. Heb. 12:6). And here, the Lord is bringing chastening first to the church. Now, those who do not belong to Him are ultimately judged for their sins, but those who are His are sanctified.

Lastly, *suffering builds faith*. In verse 19 we read, 'Therefore let those who suffer according to God's will entrust their souls to a faithful Creator while doing good.' Notice that he says, 'those who suffer according to God's will.' Now, all suffering takes place under His sovereign control. But whereas suffering that comes as a result of sin needs to produce repentance, godly suffering should build faith. He says, 'Believer, entrust your soul to the faithful Creator!' We are to draw near to the Lord and not run away. In the midst of your suffering and trials, God will work in you to grow your faith. He sharpens you. He creates bullet-proof faith. If God desires you to be like Christ, then He will bring you in to share in a measure of Christ's sufferings.

Despite what some pop culture icons tell you, Christianity is not all about being successful, powerful, victorious, and larger-than-life. That's the theology of glory. Rather it's about being humble, weak, trusting God, faithful to Him, and denying ourselves. Jesus said, 'If anyone would come after Me, let him deny himself and take up his cross daily and follow Me' (Luke 9:23). Jesus the Baptist declared, 'He must increase, but I must decrease' (John 3:30).

That's the theology of the cross.

Appendix 3
Simul Justus et Peccator
('At the same time just and sinner')

What is the Reformation all about? In the simplest sense, it was an answer to the question: *How does a person get right with God?* And in answering this question, the Reformers appealed to the highest authority—not Popes, councils, or traditions—but to the authority of Scripture alone. And what they found was that our salvation, our good relationship with God as Christians, is rooted in God's grace alone. Furthermore, we have no inherent goodness; no ability to make us 'saveable.' Rather, God takes pity on the sinner and decides to show mercy and grace. And according to Ephesians 2:8, it is 'by grace you have been saved through faith.' God enables us to hear and understand the gospel and we are called to believe it.

We put our faith in Jesus Christ, as He is the author and perfector of our faith and our salvation. The Bible does not teach that salvation comes by faith plus works, or faith plus religion, or faith plus tradition, or faith plus piety. No, it is by faith *alone* in Jesus Christ. He is our sole Savior—our salvation does not come by way of a 'team effort.' We don't have Mary and the saints and our loved ones praying for us to go to heaven—none of that has any saving power. Only Christ, and Christ alone.

Furthermore, our understanding of Christianity is not rooted in vague spirituality, or worldly wisdom, or speculation, or the victory of man (Luther called this 'the theology of glory'). Rather, we understand that the central focus is the cross of Christ. The apostle Paul declares in 1 Corinthians 2:2, 'I decided to know nothing among you except Jesus Christ and Him crucified.' God's love and justice meet perfectly at the cross. In fact, Luther professed that our Christian theology is a 'theology of the cross.'

Furthermore, our view is not simplistic or minimalistic, rather we see all the Christian life as being lived to the glory of God alone. And that there is no distinction between the clergy and the laity; between the spiritual and the super-spiritual. Every Christian man and woman is a minister of the gospel of Jesus Christ. The Reformers called this the 'priesthood of all believers' (cf. 1 Pet. 2).

And so, the Reformation isn't simply about the ancient history of the church—we're not celebrating the memory of old, dead men. Rather Christianity is alive and well because Christ is alive; resurrected and ascended. And we know this because the Word of God is 'living and active' (Heb. 4:12). This subject affects us today, right now; in real time.

The key question to consider is: *How does God save sinners today?* The short answer is, the same way He has always saved them—by grace through faith in Christ. However, when we delve deeper, we see that there is the exploration into *how* God is able to save people. After all, He is so holy, so righteous, so perfect; and we are sinful, deceitful, and unworthy. So, *how* can God save sinners?

Abraham's Justification

If you devote yourself to reading the Bible, one thing you notice is that every person named in it is a sinner (that is, all but Jesus). For example, Paul persecuted the church before his salvation, even bickering with brothers after his conversion. John, in his younger years, was a hot-head, known for wanting to call down judgment on his enemies. Peter was impetuous and unfaithful. Solomon, although the wisest man in history, was still foolish, disobeying the Lord by marrying pagan wives who would lead him astray.

David was an adulterer and a murderer. Moses was tentative and untrusting at times, while other times he was completely over-the-top. In fact, he got so angry at Israel that he struck the rock that was to provide water, disobeying the command of God, and got himself kicked out of the Promised Land before they even arrived. Jacob was a liar and a deceiver. Noah was a drunkard. And on it goes. Scripture is correct; there really are none who are righteous.

Yet when we consider the life of Abraham, we see an amazing arc to the story. Genesis 15 drops us in the middle of his story. Now, we all know Abraham as the father of Israel—the patriarch. He's the Jewish George Washington. And while he's living in the land of Ur, the Lord appears to him and tells him that he will become the father to a great nation. So, he sets out from Ur and travels to Canaan, to the future home of the Israelites.

Before he gets to Canaan, however, he makes a pit stop in Egypt and commits a gross sin. The Pharaoh sees Abram's wife, Sarai, and takes an interest in her. And Abram, out of fear of being killed, pretends that she's his sister, and allows Pharaoh to take her into his house, and into his bed. In response to the sin, God sends plagues to punish the transgression, to which Pharaoh confronts Abram, yells at him for not being forthright, and then kicks him out of Egypt. At this point, Abram's sin is proven. Of course, it's later demonstrated when Abram himself commits adultery by impregnating Hagar in an attempt to produce a child naturally.

But in Genesis 15, we see the Lord's sovereign act of justifying Abram (later named Abraham) by his faith.

> After these things the word of the Lord came to Abram in a vision: 'Fear not, Abram, I am your shield; your reward shall be very great.' But Abram said, 'O Lord God, what will you give me, for I continue childless, and the heir of my house is Eliezer of Damascus?' And Abram said, 'Behold, you have given me no offspring, and a member of my household will be my heir.' And behold, the word of the Lord came to him: 'This man shall not be

your heir; your very own son shall be your heir.' And he brought him outside and said, 'Look toward heaven, and number the stars, if you are able to number them.' Then he said to him, 'So shall your offspring be.' And he believed the LORD, and he counted it to him as righteousness (vv. 1-6).

At this point, Abram is childless, and his initial idea is that, perhaps Eliezer might be the heir, or others in his house. Frankly, he's wondering *how* God might deliver on His promise, since its fulfillment seems impossible. But God comes to him in a vision and offers comfort: 'Fear not, Abram, I am your shield; your reward shall be very great' (v. 1). Yet Abram still had concerns. How will God preserve his family? How will He save and bless them? The Lord responds in verse 4 by telling Abram that Eliezer would not be his heir. This becomes part of the Lord's promise.

Then the Lord takes Abram outside to look up at the countless number of stars. God tells him, 'Number the stars, if you are able to number them' (v. 5). Of course, Abram could not even do that! To which God says, 'So shall your offspring be.' In essence, the sentiment is, 'Not only will I give you a child of your own, but your heritage will become more numerous than all the millions of stars in the sky.' Millions and millions of descendants. And we know that this comes to pass through his grandson, Jacob, who the Lord renames 'Israel.' And the people who come through this line number into the millions, even to this day.

But God makes a supernatural promise to Abram, and he considers it. We read in verse 6, 'And he believed the Lord, and he counted it to him as righteousness.' The Hebrew word *sedaqa* can be rendered both 'righteousness' and 'justice,' but in the context, it pertains to an absolute righteousness, even honesty, truthfulness, or moral purity. In essence, this is the character of God. Now up to this point, we've seen Abram act dishonestly, unrighteously, and immorally; even afterward lapsing into sinfulness. But here in verse 6, we see that God 'counted' or considered Abram righteous, even though he's not. Yet God credits him with a righteousness that doesn't inherently belong to him.

The question then becomes, *based on what?* The answer: his faith.

Justification and Imputed Righteousness

In Paul's letter to the Romans he works meticulously through the theology of the gospel. He notes in chapter 1 verse 16, that he is 'not ashamed of the gospel, for it is the power of God for salvation to everyone who believes, to the Jew first and also to the Greek.' But before he even gets to the salvation of the sinner, he lifts up the righteousness of God, putting it on full display. In the second half of chapter 1, Paul chronicles the absolute immoral assault on the righteousness of God by the unrighteous. But such as assault is met by only one thing: God's wrath. He notes, 'For the wrath of God is revealed from heaven against all ungodliness and unrighteousness of men' (v. 18). The point is clear—all sin, all ungodliness, and all unrighteousness is punished by God. We read later that 'the wages of sin is death' (Rom. 6:23).

But then, in chapters 2 and 3, Paul addresses those who would attempt to approach God with their *own* righteousness. First, he addresses the so-called moralist—those who believe that they have some inherent goodness. His concluding sentiments in chapter 2, verses 1 through 16 are essentially, 'You may appear to be upright to others, but God will expose even your secret sins.' Then he addresses the Jew (vv. 2:17–3:8) who believes that he will be saved because of his ability to keep God's law through obedience. But Paul condemns them for their hypocrisy, noting that they continually break the laws they teach. And then, for good measure, Paul drops the hammer on everyone else in the world (3:9-20), concluding in verse 23, 'for all have sinned and fall short of the glory of God.' Nobody is just. Nobody is righteous. Everyone is a sinner. Therefore, every person is deserving of the wrath of God spelled out in Romans 1:18.

And so, we find ourselves at an impasse. How will anyone be saved? How can they be?! Paul gives the answer at the end of chapter 3, but it's important to note that Paul intends to offer Abraham to us as an illustration of *how* God can save a sinner. He writes:

> What then shall we say was gained by Abraham, our forefather according to the flesh? For if Abraham was justified by works, he has something to boast about, but not before God. For what does the Scripture say? 'Abraham believed God, and it was counted to him as righteousness.' Now to the one who works, his wages are not counted as a gift but as his due. And to the one who does not work but believes in him who justifies the ungodly, his faith is counted as righteousness (Rom. 4:1-5).

To summarize, the argument is essentially this—

What did Abraham *do* to be accepted by God? Was it based on his works or deeds?

If it were based on good deeds, then he could boast about being a good person. But we have established that that was not the case. Furthermore, if he *was* able to earn his salvation by his deeds, then God's blessing would not be a gift (grace). Rather it would have been what God owed to him. However, what does the Scripture say? We read in verse 3, 'Abraham believed God, and it was counted to him as righteousness.' Here Paul is quoting from Genesis 15:6.

And so, we see that God does not declare Abraham to be righteous because of his deeds; rather He counts him as righteous because he trusts in God. He believes Him. God makes a promise to Abraham, and he responds in his heart by saying, 'I believe You.' Then, Paul opens it up and applies the promise to all people, saying, 'And to the one who does not work but believes in him who justifies the ungodly, his faith is counted as righteousness' (v. 5). The key phrase for our purposes is '[God] justifies the ungodly.'

Later in Romans 5 Paul points to the fact that God saved us 'while we were still sinners' (v. 8) and 'while we were enemies'

(v. 10). Ephesians 2:1 notes, 'And you were dead in the trespasses and sins in which you once walked.' Further, 'even when we were dead in our trespasses, God made us alive together with Christ— for by grace you have been saved' (v. 5). How is God able to do this? He can do it because of what is known as *imputed righteousness*.

Jesus Christ, who is perfectly righteous, died in our place on the cross. He is punished by God in our place as a substitute. In the same moment that Christ dies, God 'imputes' or considers our sin as belonging to Christ (even though He is sinless). At the exact same time, He credits us with Christ's own righteousness (even though we are unrighteous). And the key element at work is our *faith* in Jesus Christ enabled by the grace of God. This is how Paul can make the statement in Romans 3:26 that 'God is just … and the justifier of the one who has faith in Jesus.'

This strange dichotomy is what led Martin Luther to begin using the Latin phrase: *simul justus et peccātor*. The word *simul* is the root of our English word 'simultaneous.' *Justus* refers to justice or righteousness. *Et* simply means 'and.' *Peccātor* means 'sinner.' Put together the Latin phrase is rendered: 'At the same time just and sinner.'

Earlier in his life, Luther held to an earlier Augustinian view that we are partly sinful and partly just. But in reading the Bible, we see that it is impossible to conclude that we are anything except sinful. Yet when God declares a person to be justified, there's no lesser degree—we're as justified as we'll ever need to be. It's one or the other. In fact, later in his life, Luther further modified his phrase and maintained: *semper justus et peccātor*—'always just and always sinner.' There's never a time when you're partly anything, whether sinful or just. It's all or nothing.

And because we are ever sinful, we can't think that our doing good deeds gives God any reason to save us. This is akin to a mass-murderer standing before the judge in court and pleading his case saying, 'At least I didn't break the speed limit on the way to the crime scene,' as if his small act of virtue could somehow offset his greater sins. But we often reason this way, arguing to God that our meager deeds of goodness somehow balance out our life of sin.

But the only way God can reconcile us to Himself is by '[counting] Him, who knew no sin [Christ], to be sinful, so that we might know the righteousness of God in Him' (2 Cor. 5:21). Because of Jesus Christ, God considers us righteous and acceptable for heaven, even though we are otherwise deserving of hell.

Where does this leave us?

Responding to God's Grace

Christians often struggle with regard to assurance. They become confused and downtrodden. They question their salvation. They convince themselves that their sins somehow disinherit them from the love of God. Now, for those who would assume that the cross of Christ gives them license to sin, they ought to take a long, hard look at their life and prayerfully weep through 1 John. But for those who truly love God, but are plagued with the guilt and shame over sin, they need to know that they are justified—declared righteous— not because of how good they *can be*, but because of how good God *is* to justify us by our faith in Christ.

And with faith, there is also the repentance of sin. In short, repentance is the changing of one's mind to align with God with regard to sin, and purposing to go in a different direction. And a Christian who understands justification has more boldness, more strength, and more confidence in Christ to wage war on their sin. Justification, then, becomes the bedrock platform by which we are launched into sanctification. Justification is like the starting block, used by sprinters to launch themselves into the race. It's the foundation and strength in the Christian life.

But this is not something we do for ourselves. We are saved and justified by God's grace alone, by faith alone, in Christ alone—not of ourselves; it is the gift of God.

What is to be our posture before God?

In Luke 18, Jesus illustrates the posture of humility and repentance before God through a parable. He explains,

> 'Two men went up into the temple to pray, one a Pharisee and the other a tax collector. The Pharisee, standing by himself, prayed thus: "God, I thank you that I am not like other men, extortioners, unjust, adulterers, or even like this tax collector. I fast twice a week; I give tithes of all that I get." But the tax collector, standing far off, would not even lift up his eyes to heaven, but beat his breast, saying, "God, be merciful to me, a sinner!" I tell you, this man went down to his house justified, rather than the other. For everyone who exalts himself will be humbled, but the one who humbles himself will be exalted' (Luke 18:10-14).

We are all sinners, which will never change until we get to heaven. Yet we are repentant sinners. But, by God's grace, at the same time, we are counted righteous in Christ. Both realities are true. And it is because of that 'great exchange'—the guilt of our sins for the merit of Christ's righteousness—that we are made right with God.

May we never forget that.

Acknowledgments

More and more, I'm becoming convinced that very few people do anything of any true value by themselves. Writing is no exception. Throughout this project, I've had the support and input of many people.

First, my deep thanks to Harvest Bible Church who allowed me the privilege of teaching through this material on Sunday morning. Thank you to those who helped me publish the original edition (John Manning, Stephen Melniszyn, and Jill Cox), as well as the wonderful staff at Christian Focus Publishing for the new edition, namely William MacKenzie, Rosanna Burton, and Anne Norrie.

Jess, my lovely and godly wife, was the first person I 'pitched' and who gave me the green light for *Why We're Protestant*—she is ever a source of strength, stimulation, and support. I love you, my dear! My kids are too young to read this right now, but someday I hope they'll forgive me for 'working ... *again*?!'

All thanks must be given to our great God and Savior Jesus Christ, for sovereignly superintending my way, and allowing me the blessing of preaching, teaching, and writing. Lord, You are the Author of sound doctrine; You are why we're anything. Thank You for calling me out of darkness and into Your marvelous light.

Recommended Resources

INTRODUCTORY/GENERAL

Allison, Gregg R. *40 Questions About Roman Catholicism.* (Grand Rapids: Kregel, 2021).

Bainton, Roland H. *Here I Stand: A Life of Martin Luther.* (Peabody: Hendrickson, 1950).

Gendron, Mike. *Preparing for Eternity: Should we trust God's Word or Religious Traditions?* (Plano: PTG, 2011).

Godfrey, W. Robert. *John Calvin: Pilgrim and Pastor.* (Wheaton: Crossway, 2009).

Johnson, Terry L. *The Case for Traditional Protestantism: The Solas of the Reformation.* (Edinburgh: Banner of Truth Trust, 2004).

Nichols, Stephen J. *Martin Luther: A Guided Tour of His Life and Thought.* (Phillipsburg: P&R, 2002).

Reeves, Michael & Chester, Tim. *Why the Reformation Still Matters.* (Wheaton: Crossway, 2016).

Sproul, R.C. *Are We Together? A Protestant Analyzes Roman Catholicism.* (Grand Rapids: Baker, 1995).

_____. *Faith Alone: The Evangelical Doctrine of Justification.* (Orlando: Reformation Trust, 2012).

ADVANCED

Allison, Gregg R. *Roman Catholic Theology & Practice: An Evangelical Assessment.* (Wheaton: Crossway, 2014).

Barrett, Matthew. *God's Word Alone: The Authority of Scripture.* (The Five Solas Series. Grand Rapids: Zondervan, 2016).

Barrett, Matthew, ed. *Reformation Theology: A Systematic Summary.* (Wheaton: Crossway, 2017).

George, Timothy. *Theology of the Reformers.* (Nashville, B&H, 2013).

Gordon, Bruce. *Calvin.* (New Haven: Yale University Press, 2009).

Luther, Martin. *Bondage of the Will*, trans. J.I. Packer and O.R. Johnson. 1525; (reprint, London: James Clark & Co. Ltd., 1957).

_____. *Three Treatises.* (Philadelphia: Fortress, 1970).

Schreiner, Thomas. *Faith Alone: The Doctrine of Justification.* (The Five Solas Series. Grand Rapids: Zondervan, 2015).

Trueman, Carl R. *Grace Alone: Salvation as a Gift of God.* The Five Solas Series. (Grand Rapids: Zondervan, 2017).

Vandrunen, David. *God's Glory Alone: The Majestic Heart of the Christian Faith and Life.* The Five Solas Series. (Grand Rapids: Zondervan, 2015).

Wellum, Stephan. *Christ Alone: The Uniqueness of Jesus as Savior.* The Five Solas Series. (Grand Rapids: Zondervan, 2017).

White, James R. *Scripture Alone: Exploring the Bible's Accuracy, Authority, and Authenticity.* (Minneapolis: Bethany House, 2004).

_____. *The Roman Catholic Controversy.* (Minneapolis: Harvest House, 1996).

Why we need the Church
(and why the Church needs us)

WHO NEEDS THE
CHURCH?

TERRY JOHNSON

ISBN: 978-1-5271-0835-6

Who Needs the Church?
Why We Need the Church, and the Church Needs Us
by Terry L. Johnson

A thought–provoking introduction to the importance of the local church.

It seems that increasing numbers of professing Christians in the West do not attend church. Church, to many, has become a place to go when it is convenient, to have one's needs met. Terry L. Johnson asks whether our individualistic, dismissive attitude to the gathering of the local church can be squared with that of the New Testament.

Examining what the Bible has to say about the church, Johnson shows why the local body of believers is an essential part of the life of every believer – and the role that each individual believer plays in the life of the church. This thought–provoking, challenging book will benefit every believer.

Terry L. Johnson
Terry Johnson is the senior minister of the Independent Presbyterian Church in Savannah, Georgia, which he has served since 1987.

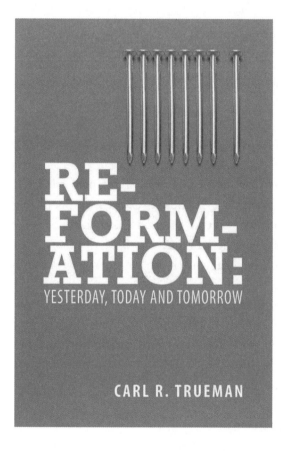

ISBN: 978-1-84550-701-5

Reformation

Yesterday, Today and Tomorrow
by Carl Trueman

Carl R. Trueman examines the origins of contemporary Reformed theology in the Reformation world of the sixteenth and seventeenth centuries. After tracing how this heritage shaped and transformed the intervening period, he then describes some of the major challenges being faced by the evangelical church at the present time, and suggests ways of responding which remain faithful to the Scriptures and the theology of the Reformers drawn from it, and points towards a future that embraces and disseminates these wonderful doctrines of grace.

Carl R. Trueman

Carl Trueman is Professor of Biblical and Religious Studies at Grove City College, Pennsylvania. He was previously Paul Woolley Professor of Historical Theology and Church History at Westminster Theological Seminary, Philadelphia, Pennsylvania. He has contributed to the Dictionary of Historical Theology, the Dictionary of National Biography, The Cambridge Companion to Reformation Theology and the Blackwell Companion to Modern Theology.

Compiled by Andrew Cook

The
Reformation
A Sound-bite History

ISBN: 978-1-78191-986-6

The Reformation
A Sound-bite History
compiled by Andrew Cook

- An introduction
- Written in an easy-to-read style
- Captures the essence of the Reformation

In honour of the 500-year anniversary of the Reformation, this small book goes through some of the key events and characters who, under God, brought about one of the most significant changes in the history of the church. Covering great names, such as Luther, and less well-known names, such as John Huss, this work seeks to present the essence and impact of this great era. This is an engaging and accessible introduction to the Reformation.

Andrew Cook
Andrew Cook oversees production of Serving Today, the Grace Baptist Mission radio programme for pastors and church leaders. He has been with the GBM radio team since 2004.

Christian Focus Publications

Our mission statement –

STAYING FAITHFUL

In dependence upon God we seek to impact the world through literature faithful to His infallible Word, the Bible. Our aim is to ensure that the Lord Jesus Christ is presented as the only hope to obtain forgiveness of sin, live a useful life and look forward to heaven with Him.

Our books are published in four imprints:

CHRISTIAN
FOCUS

Popular works including biographies, commentaries, basic doctrine and Christian living.

CHRISTIAN
HERITAGE

Books representing some of the best material from the rich heritage of the church.

MENTOR

Books written at a level suitable for Bible College and seminary students, pastors, and other serious readers. The imprint includes commentaries, doctrinal studies, examination of current issues and church history.

CF4•K

Children's books for quality Bible teaching and for all age groups: Sunday school curriculum, puzzle and activity books; personal and family devotional titles, biographies and inspirational stories – because you are never too young to know Jesus!

Christian Focus Publications Ltd,
Geanies House, Fearn, Ross-shire,
IV20 1TW, Scotland, United Kingdom.
www.christianfocus.com